9.95

Doorway
to
Creative Cuisine

by
Nila Hoolaeff

Doorway to Creative Cuisine

By Nila Hoolaeff

First Printing — December, 1984

Copyright © 1984 by
Doorway to Creative Cuisine Publishing
R.R. #1, Site 25
Compartment 1
Castlegar, B.C.
V1N 3H7

Canadian Cataloguing in Publication Data

Hoolaeff, Nila
  Doorway to creative cuisine

Includes index.
ISBN 0-919845-22-3

1. Cookery.   2. Cookery, International
3. Vegetarian cookery   I. Title

TX 715.H65 1984   641.5   C85-091034-X

Food Photography by
Keith Holuboff, Vancouver, B.C.

Photograph Back Cover by
Michael of Vogue, Castlegar, B.C.

Design by Blair Fraser

Designed, Printed, and Produced in Canada by
Centax of Canada
1048 Fleury Street
Regina, Saskatchewan, Canada S4N 4W8

#105 - 4711 13 Street N.E.
Calgary, Alberta, Canada T2E 6M3

Table Of Contents

Introduction

The sharing of food has always been to me a serious and joyful proposition. Feeding people lovingly and graciously is one of life's simplest pleasures.

I delight in the thought that, in our home, friends and relatives always feel welcome and always leave refreshed. Sharing food is a large part of this, and I enjoy planning and preparing meals for them.

This book is composed of my favorite recipes, which I have collected and adapted throughout the years from relatives and friends. Most of the recipes can be adapted to a vegetarian lifestyle by substituting or eliminating the broth or the meat.

I would like to add a special note of thanks to my family and friends for the encouragement and support they gave me to get my book started and on its way. They have also thoroughly tested all of my recipes with great appreciation. I offer my recipes now to you to share with your family and friends. Enjoy! And always add a dash of love.

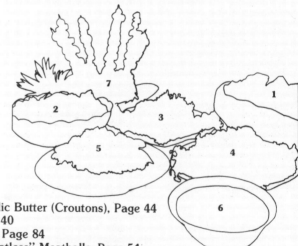

Front Cover

1. French Bread, Garlic Butter (Croutons), Page 44
2. Greek Salad, Page 40
3. Home-Style Tacos, Page 84
4. Spaghetti and "Meatless" Meatballs, Page 54
5. Stir-Fry Garden Vegetables On Rice, Page 99
6. Summer Borscht, Page 69
7. Yakatori, Page 94

Appetizers

Cheese Ball

16 oz. cream cheese, softened
4 cloves garlic, minced
2 tbsp. diced green pepper
2 tbsp. diced celery
½ cup chopped green onion
½ cup finely diced onion
1 tbsp. snipped parsley
1 tsp. Worcestershire sauce
1 tsp. paprika
1 tsp. seasoned salt
1 tsp. lemon pepper
.37 oz. pkg. (2 tbsp.) mixed spices salad dressing
24 oz. shredded cheese (two or more of white, yellow, mozzarella, Cheddar)
½ cup mayonnaise garnish (see below)

Beat well everything except grated cheese. Add cheese. If too thick, thin with ¼ cup sour cream, buttermilk or milk. Shape into 3 small balls or 1 large. Roll in toasted chopped almonds, walnuts, sesame seeds, paprika, or snipped parsley. Serve with crackers. See photograph page 16.

Cheese Tarts

Pastry for 2 - crust 9" pie
1 cup grated Swiss cheese
1½ cups milk, scalded
3 eggs, beaten
½ tsp. salt
⅛ tsp. nutmeg
dash pepper
paprika

Heat oven to 375°F. Roll out pastry and cut into 3" rounds. Line 36 - 2" tart pans with pastry rounds. Sprinkle a generous teaspoonful of grated cheese into each tart. Combine milk, eggs, salt, nutmeg and pepper and spoon this mixture into tarts over the cheese, filling each tart about ⅔ full. Sprinkle lightly with paprika. Bake about 15 minutes or until pastry is well browned and filling is set. Serve warm. Makes 36 tarts.

Cheese Squares

1 loaf unsliced bread
½ lb. room temperature
   butter
¼ lb. grated Cheddar
   cheese

1 egg white
¼ tsp. salt
½ tsp. paprika
1 tbsp. cream
1 tsp. garlic powder

Remove crusts and cut bread into 1½" cubes. Beat all ingredients until fluffy. Spread on cubes, arrange on flat tray and freeze. Store in bag. When needed arrange on cookie sheet. Bake at 350°F until brown. See photograph page 16.

Bourbon Wieners

1 cup brown sugar
1 cup bourbon whiskey

14 oz. ketchup
12 wieners

Simmer sugar, whiskey and ketchup for 2 hours. Let stand 24 hours before using. When serving, slice wieners diagonally into 4 pieces. Simmer in sauce for ½ hour before serving. Serve in chafing dish.

Stuffed Mushrooms

1 lb. mushrooms
1 cup chopped onions
1 tbsp. butter
½ tsp. each salt, pepper
   and garlic salt

1 cup crushed cracker
   crumbs
3 tbsp. mayonnaise
3 tbsp. cream cheese,
   softened

Stem mushrooms, setting caps aside, and chop stems. Fry onion and mushroom stems in butter, season with spices. Remove from stove and add cracker crumbs, mayonnaise and cream cheese. Stuff mushroom caps. Bake 20 minutes at 375°F. See photograph page 16.

Mushroom Tarts

2 tbsp. soft butter
1 loaf brown bread,
   thinly sliced
4 tbsp. butter
3 tbsp. chopped green
   onion
½ lb. mushrooms,
   chopped
2 tbsp. flour

1 cup cream
½ tsp. salt
⅛ tsp. pepper
1 tsp. lemon juice
1 tbsp. chopped chives
   or green onions
4 tbsp. Parmesan
   cheese

Butter insides of smallest type of muffin tin. Cut the slices of bread into 3" rounds and press into the muffin tins. Bake in 400°F oven for 10 minutes. For the filling, melt the 4 tbsp. butter, add the onions and cook until transparent. Add the mushrooms and fry until moisture evaporates. Mix in flour. Stir in cream, bring to a boil and simmer until thickened. Add all seasonings, let cool. Fill the bread forms with this mixture and top with a sprinkling of Parmesan cheese. Bake in 350°F oven for 10 minutes. The bread forms freeze well and can be filled without defrosting. See photograph page 16.

Mushroom Surprise

1 lb. fresh large
   mushroom caps
1 egg, well beaten
½ cup flour

2 cups finely crushed
   soda crackers
½ tsp. each salt, pepper
   and garlic powder
½ cup butter

Dip mushrooms into beaten egg, then into flour, then egg again, then crumbs combined with spices. Fry in melted butter on all sides 15 minutes or until done. Serve immediately.

Mushroom Turnovers

Crust

9 oz. cream cheese, softened

½ cup butter

1½ cups flour

Mix cheese and butter, add flour and mix well. Refrigerate 2 hours, or 1 hour in freezer. Cut into 3 pieces and roll out. Cut in 3" circles with round cutter. Fill with 1½ tbsp. cooked filling. Pinch together, put on tray and freeze, then put in plastic pail or bags. When ready to use take out about 1 hour before to thaw. Prick with fork and brush with beaten egg. Bake at 400°F 15 to 20 minutes.

Filling:

1 lb. fresh mushrooms OR 4 cans mushrooms, drained

2 tbsp. butter

1 large onion

salt and pepper to taste

1/16 tsp. thyme

¼ cup sour cream

2 tbsp. flour

Finely chop mushrooms and onion. Fry mushrooms in butter, add onion and spices and fry a bit more. Gradually add flour and sour cream and mix well. Cool.

Asparagus Roll Ups

24 white or brown bread slices

16 oz. cream cheese, softened

10 oz. can asparagus, drained

2 tbsp. green onion, finely chopped

2 tbsp. mayonnaise

Cut crusts off bread slices. Flatten with rolling pin. Mash asparagus and combine with cheese, onions and mayonnaise. Spread on flattened bread slices and roll up. Freeze on cookie sheet. When needed slice into ½" rounds or leave full size and put under broiler. See photograph page 16.

Bacon & Mushroom Roll Ups

4 slices bacon, diced
2½ cups finely chopped
   mushrooms
1 onion, chopped

4 oz. cream cheese
15 slices sandwich
   bread
¼ cup butter, melted

Fry bacon, mushrooms and onions for 5 to 8 minutes or until tender but not crisp. Stir in cheese until melted and set aside. Trim crusts from bread and flatten slices slightly with rolling pin. Spread each slice with about 2 tbsp. mushroom mixture and roll up jelly-roll fashion; secure with toothpick. Place, seam side down on baking sheet. Cover and chill for at least 1 hour or freeze in single layer, then package in airtight containers. (If frozen, let stand at room temperature for 30 minutes before baking.)

Brush rolls with melted butter. Bake in 375°F oven for 10 to 15 minutes or until lightly browned. Remove toothpicks, cut rolls in half and serve warm. Makes 30 appetizers.

Bacon and Onion Snacks

6 slices cooked bacon,
   crumbled
2 cups flour
1 pkg. dry onion soup
   mix

½ cup butter
¼ cup shortening
2 eggs, beaten
2 tbsp. water

Combine bacon, flour and soup mix. Cut in butter and shortening until mixture is in coarse crumbs. Blend water and eggs, sprinkle on crumbs, and mix just until well blended. Shape into walnut-sized balls. Place well apart on ungreased cookie sheets. Flatten each with floured glass bottom. Bake 10 to 15 minutes in 400°F oven. Makes 2½ dozen.

Hiawathas

1 cup soft butter or
   margarine
8 oz. cream cheese,
   softened
1 tsp. salt

3 cups sifted all-
   purpose flour
1 cup chopped,
   toasted, blanched
   almonds

Cream butter, cream cheese, and salt together until smooth. Work in flour with spoon until mixture holds together. Shape into a ball. Heat oven to 400°F. Roll pastry ⅛" thick on sheet of heavy-duty aluminum foil. Cut pastry and foil together with scissors into 1½" x 3" rectangles. Moisten ends with water; pinch together; spread out slightly to form little canoes. Prick pastry well with fork to keep it in shape. Place on cookie sheet. Bake 13 to 15 minutes or until golden; remove foil. Canoes may be wrapped and frozen up to 2 weeks before the party. Fill with Chicken Almond Filling (below).

Sprinkle with almonds. Bake at 375°F for 10 minutes. Serve hot. Makes about 5 dozen.

Chicken Almond Filling

2 cups chopped,
   cooked chicken
½ cup minced celery
½ tsp. onion salt

2 tbsp. lemon juice
¼ cup mayonnaise or
   salad dressing

Combine chicken, celery, onion salt, and lemon juice. Add mayonnaise or salad dressing. Spoon into baked pastry canoes.

"After 30, a body has a mind of its own."

Turkey or Ham Pastries

Pastry:

5 cups all-purpose flour	1 egg
1 tbsp. brown sugar	2 tsp. vinegar
1 tsp. salt	1 egg
½ tsp. baking powder	1 tbsp. water
1 lb. lard	poppy, sesame, or caraway seeds
¾ cup cold water	

Measure flour, without sifting, into large mixing bowl. Add brown sugar, salt and baking powder; stir well to blend. Add half the lard and rub in with finger tips. Cut in remaining lard until particles are the size of small peas. Combine water, egg and vinegar in small bowl. Beat slightly. Add all at once to flour mixture and stir with fork until dough holds together. Form into a ball and wrap in waxed paper. Chill before using. Roll out portions of the dough on lightly floured surface to ⅛" thickness. Cut into circles using 3¾" or 4" cutter. Place circles on ungreased baking sheets. Spread a scant tbsp. of filling on ½ of each circle. Moisten edge and fold over. Seal edges with tines of fork. Cut slits in tops of pastries for steam to escape. Brush pastries with mixture of 1 egg beaten with 1 tbsp. water. Sprinkle poppy, caraway or sesame seeds over top if desired. Bake at 400°F for 15-20 minutes or until golden. Serve warm. See photograph page 16.

Filling:

3 cups finely diced, cooked ham or turkey	1 tbsp. minced onion
2 tbsp. chopped green pepper	2 tbsp. diced celery
2 tbsp. chopped pimiento	10½ oz. can undiluted cream of mushroom soup

Combine all ingredients, mixing well.

Saucy Cocktail Meatballs

1 lb. ground beef
2 tbsp. bread crumbs
1 egg, slightly beaten
½ tsp. salt
⅓ cup finely chopped green pepper
⅓ cup finely chopped onion
2 tbsp. butter or margarine

10 oz. can Campbell's condensed tomato soup
2 tbsp. brown sugar
4 tsp. Worcestershire sauce
1 tbsp. prepared mustard
1 tbsp. vinegar

Mix beef, crumbs, egg, salt. Shape into 50 meatballs. Place in 13" x 9" x 2" baking pan. Broil until browned; turn once. Spoon off fat. In saucepan, cook pepper and onion in butter until tender. Stir in remaining ingredients. Pour over meatballs. Cover and bake 350°F for 20 minutes.

Les Escargots

1 or 2 - 7 oz. cans escargots
½ cup butter
1 head (10 cloves) garlic, minced

1 tbsp. chopped parsley
1 dash cayenne
1 tsp. lemon juice

Sauté garlic in butter, add parsley, cayenne, lemon juice. Drain escargots and add to butter. Heat through. Let stand until ready to serve so garlic flavor will go through. Reheat. Serve with garlic bread slices. See photograph page 16.

Forty is the old age of youth; fifty is the youth of old age.

Cream Cheese Dip

1 cup sour cream
8 oz. cream cheese
3 tbsp. lemon juice
2 cloves, garlic, minced

2 green onions, finely diced
1 tsp. vegetable salt
1 tsp. lemon pepper

Cream, sour cream, cheese, and lemon juice together. Add garlic and green onions. Add spices according to taste.

Potato Skin Crisps

baked potato skins
melted butter

seasoning (see below)

Cut the leftover baked potato skins into strips or small squares with kitchen shears. Place skin side down in a single layer on a baking sheet and brush inside of skins with melted butter. Sprinkle with seasoned salt, seasoned pepper, garlic salt or whatever flavor you fancy. Bake at 350°F for 15 to 20 minutes until skins are brown and crisp. Serve as a crunchy surprise with drinks or as a crisp tidbit with soup. See photograph page 16.

Marinated Beets

8 cups cooked beets
   sliced ⅛" thick
6 cloves garlic, minced
3 large onions, sliced
   in rings
1 cup grated Parmesan
   cheese

garlic salt
3 cups salad oil
1½ cups apple cider
   vinegar
2 tbsp. salt

In a covered container like an ice cream pail alternate layers of beets, garlic, onion rings and Parmesan cheese mixed with garlic salt. Combine dressing of oil, vinegar and salt. Pour over top. Marinate. Refrigerate up to 1 month. See photograph page 16.

Breakfasts
and Brunches

Cheesy Eggs in Toast Cups

butter or margarine, softened
12 slices white bread
4 tbsp. butter
¼ cup flour
2⅓ cups milk
salt and white pepper to taste

2 tbsp. dry sherry (optional)
2 cups shredded Cheddar cheese
8 hard-cooked eggs, sliced
paprika (optional)

Grease 12 muffin pan cups lightly with butter. Trim crusts from bread. (Dry crusts and save for stuffing or bread crumbs). Fit 1 slice bread into each muffin cup and toast in preheated 400°F oven 10 minutes, or until golden brown. Melt 4 tbsp. butter in large saucepan. With whisk stir in flour until blended, then gradually stir in milk, beating briskly to prevent lumps. Cook until thickened. Season with salt, pepper and sherry. Stir in cheese and cook and stir until melted. Gently fold in egg slices and heat. Taste sauce and adjust seasonings. Just before serving, arrange 1 or 2 toast cups on each plate and fill with egg mixture. Sprinkle with paprika. Makes about 6 servings.

Egg Nests

2 slices hot buttered toast
2 slices ham (optional)
2 slices process cheese

2 eggs
¼ tsp. salt
1 tsp. butter
pepper

Preheat oven to 350°F. Place toast on baking sheet. Top each slice with ham, if desired, and cheese. Separate eggs, keeping yolks in half of the shell for later use. Beat egg whites and salt until stiff but not dry. Divide evenly and pile whites on toast slices. With back of spoon make an indentation in the center of each pile of egg white. Carefully put an egg yolk into each indentation. Place ½ tsp. butter on top of each yolk. Sprinkle with pepper. Bake 12 to 15 minutes. Serve at once with sliced tomatoes.

Cottage Cheese Pancakes

6 eggs, separated
2 cups dry cottage
  cheese
½ cup sour cream

1 cup flour
2 tsp. baking powder
1 tsp. salt
⅛ tsp. cream of tartar
  oil or butter for frying

Beat together the egg yolks, cottage cheese, sour cream, flour, baking powder, and salt. In another bowl beat the egg whites with the cream of tartar until they are stiff but not dry. Fold the beaten whites gently into the cheese mixture. Drop the batter by large spoonfuls onto an oiled griddle or skillet. Fry the pancakes until golden brown on both sides and puffy. Serve at once with sour cream, preserves, honey, apple butter or powdered sugar. OR, instead of making pancakes, fold batter into well-buttered 2-quart casserole dish and bake at 350°F 25 to 30 minutes. Serve with melted butter.

Millet Pancakes

4 eggs, separated
2 cups buttermilk
2 cups cooked millet*
1 tsp. salt
¾ tsp. soda

2 tsp. baking powder
2 heaping tsp. rice
  polishings
1 tbsp. wheat germ
1½ cups flour

Beat whites until stiff. Put everything else into blender and beat well. Fold in whites. Make pancakes on greased griddle. *The night before, soak 1 cup millet in 2 cups water. Bring to a boil, shut heat off and let stand until morning. OR the night before put 1 cup millet into thermos bottle, fill with 2 cups boiling water, and let stand till morning.

Easter Egg Pancakes

2 cups sifted all-
   purpose flour
1 tsp. salt
1 tsp. baking soda
1½ tbsp. sugar

2 eggs, lightly beaten
2 cups buttermilk
2 tbsp. butter or
   margarine, melted

Sift together into a bowl flour, salt, baking soda, and sugar. Add remaining ingredients; stir just enough to moisten flour mixture. Batter will not be smooth. Heat griddle until it is hot enough to make a drop of cold water dance. Then lightly grease it. Use a measuring cup to pour about ½ cup batter onto center of griddle. Spread lightly with the back of a spoon to form a circle about 7" in diameter. Cook over low heat until cake is full of broken bubbles. With a broad spatula or pancake turner, loosen and turn to brown other side. Keep warm between layers of paper towels in a 200°F oven. Follow same steps for each pancake. Stack 4 or 5 pancakes with Easter Egg Sauce, (recipe follows) between each layer and on top. To serve, cut in pie-shaped wedges. Serve additional sauce.

Easter Egg Sauce

¼ cup butter or
   margarine
¼ cup flour
¾ tsp. salt
⅛ tsp. pepper

1½ tsp. prepared
   mustard
2 cups milk
6 eggs, hard-cooked
⅓ cup pimiento-stuffed
   olives

In saucepan, melt butter over low heat. Blend in flour and remove from heat. Add salt, pepper, and mustard. Stir in milk gradually. Cook over low heat, stirring constantly until sauce thickens, and boils for 1 minute. Slice eggs and olives and add to sauce. Cover and keep warm while preparing pancakes.

Potato Latkes

4 potatoes, peeled
1 small onion
2 eggs
2 tbsp. flour

1 tsp. salt
¼ tsp. white pepper
vegetable oil
cheese, sliced

Finely grate potatoes into a large bowl. Grate onion into bowl. Drain off excess potato liquid. Beat in eggs, then stir in flour, salt and pepper. Heat about ¼" oil in a large skillet. Drop potato mixture by tablespoonfuls into hot oil. Brown just until edges are crisp; turn and brown other side. To browned side add a slice of your favorite cheese while other side browns.

Eggs In Mushroom Sauce

1 lb. fresh mushrooms
¼ cup butter
1 tbsp. grated onion
¼ cup flour
½ tsp. salt

¼ tsp. pepper
2 cups light cream
6 eggs
salt
pepper
grated Parmesan
cheese

Heat oven to 350°F. Wash and slice mushrooms. Heat butter in heavy saucepan, add mushrooms and onion, and cook 5 minutes. Sprinkle in flour, the ½ tsp. salt and ¼ tsp. pepper, and let bubble up. Remove from heat. Add cream all at once to mushroom mixture. Stir to blend and return to moderate heat. Cook, stirring constantly, until thick and smooth. Spoon sauce into 6 individual greased custard cups. Make a hollow in the center of the sauce with the back of a large spoon and drop an egg into each hollow. Sprinkle lightly with salt and pepper. Bake at 350°F until eggs are nearly set, about 15 minutes. Remove from oven and turn on broiler. Sprinkle the yolk of each egg generously with grated Parmesan cheese and slip under broiler for 1 minute to brown cheese lightly. Serves 6.

Bechamel Balls

Walnut Balls:

1½ cups ground walnuts
4 oz. grated Cheddar
½ cup bread crumbs
½ cup wheat germ
½ onion, minced or
    grated
¾ cup milk

2 tbsp. snipped parsley
freshly ground
    pepper
salt
3 cups Bechamel sauce
2 eggs, well beaten

In a large bowl, mix together ground walnuts, finely grated cheese, breadcrumbs, wheat germ, minced onion, and the milk. Season the mixture with chopped parsley, a lot of freshly ground pepper, and some salt. Add the well beaten eggs. Roll the mixture into balls slightly smaller than eggs. Arrange them in a buttered baking dish. Make Bechamel sauce (below) and pour it over the walnut balls in the baking dish. Bake 375°F for 35 to 40 minutes. Serve hot from baking dish.

Bechamel Sauce:

2 tbsp. butter
2 tbsp. flour
1½ cups milk, scalded

⅛ tsp. pepper
⅛ tsp. thyme
1 tbsp. dry onion soup
    mix

Melt butter, blend in flour and cook slowly over low heat for 2 minutes, stirring constantly. Remove from heat and add hot milk and seasonings. Beat vigorously with a wire whisk. Return to heat and boil 1 minute, stirring constantly.

Cheerfulness and content are great beautifiers, and are famous preservers of youthful looks.

Mile High Omelette Souffle

2 tbsp. butter
10 oz. can sliced
   mushrooms,
   drained
6-10 eggs, separated
½ pkg. onion soup mix
   (or 1 tsp. seasoned
   salt, plus pepper to
   taste)

3 tbsp. flour
1 tsp. baking powder
1 cup milk
2 cups grated Cheddar
   cheese

Heat large electric frying pan to 300°F. Melt butter in pan. Add mushrooms and fry. Meanwhile separate eggs. Beat whites stiff. Then beat yolks and add onion soup mix (OR seasoned salt and pepper) flour, baking powder, and milk. Beat well, then fold in whites. Gently pour over mushrooms. Seal tightly with lid and do not open for 10 to 15 minutes. Sprinkle Cheddar cheese over omelette, close lid again, and cook until melted, 5 more minutes. To serve cut in family portions and lift out with pancake lifter. Serve with toast.

Spanish Sauce for Omelettes

½ cup butter
½ cup chopped onions
2 cloves garlic, minced
1 green pepper, diced
10 oz. can sliced
   mushrooms,
   drained
1 stalk celery, diced

1 qt. tomatoes
   salt and pepper to
   taste
2 tbsp. butter
   your favorite plain
    omelette recipe
   grated cheese

In butter, fry onions, garlic, green pepper, mushrooms, celery, tomatoes, salt and pepper. Sauté until thickened. Melt 2 tbsp. butter in covered frying pan. Make omelette and gently pour into pan. Dot 2 cups sauce by tablespoon here and there. Close lid and cook 15 minutes. Sprinkle with grated cheese just before serving.

Brunch Egg Casserole

2 cups plain croutons
1 cup shredded
   Cheddar cheese
4 eggs, lightly beaten
2 cups milk
½ tsp. salt

½ tsp. prepared
   mustard
⅛ tsp. onion powder
   pepper to taste
4 slices bacon
   bacon curls
   (optional)

In bottom of greased 10" x 6" x 1¾" baking dish, combine croutons and Cheddar cheese. In a bowl, combine eggs, milk, salt, prepared mustard, onion powder, and pepper; mix until blended. Pour over crouton mixture in casserole. Cook 4 slices bacon until crisp; drain and crumble. Sprinkle over top of casserole and bake in 325°F oven for 55 to 60 minutes or until eggs are set. Garnish with bacon curls, if desired. Makes 6 servings.

Eggs A La Asparagus

3 tbsp. butter
3 tbsp. all-purpose
   flour
½ tsp. salt
   dash pepper
2 cups milk
½ cup sharp cheese
   grated

4 hard-cooked eggs,
   sliced
10 oz. pkgs. frozen
   asparagus, cooked
   and drained
4 slices toast
   paprika

In 2-quart saucepan, melt butter over low heat; blend in flour, salt and pepper. Add milk all at once; cook, stirring constantly, until mixture thickens and bubbles. Add cheese; stir until melted. Fold in egg slices. Arrange hot asparagus spears on toast. Pour egg mixture over asparagus. Sprinkle with paprika. Makes 4 servings.

Mushroom Puff

10 oz. can mushroom
   pieces, drained
1 cup grated Cheddar
   cheese

2 eggs, beaten
½ tsp. dry mustard
1 tsp. baking powder
4 slices toast

Combine cheese and mushrooms. Beat eggs with spices and baking powder. Stir into cheese-mushroom mixture. Spread ¼ of mixture on each piece of toast. Broil 5 minutes.

Creamed Saucy Eggs

1 large onion, chopped
½ cup butter
10 oz. mushrooms,
   sliced
¼ cup flour
½ tsp. salt

¼ tsp. pepper
1 tbsp. dry onion soup
   mix
1 cup milk
6 eggs
1-2 cups grated cheese

Fry onion in butter. Add mushrooms. Sauté 2 minutes more. Beat flour, salt, pepper, onion soup, milk and eggs well. Pour into onion-mushroom mixture and cook until thickened. Add shredded cheese. Stir until melted. Spoon over toast.

Denver Omelette

½ pkg. bacon OR 1 cup
   diced ham
1 cup diced onions
1 green pepper, diced
10 oz. mushrooms,
   sliced

6-8 eggs
1 cup cream
½ tsp. salt
¼ tsp. pepper
6 slices toast

Dice bacon or ham and fry till crisp. Drain fat from pan. To bacon add diced onion, pepper and mushrooms. Sauté well. Beat eggs with cream, salt and pepper. Pour over bacon mixture, stirring until eggs set. Serve over toast.

Western Rarebit

½ cup finely chopped
  celery
⅓ cup finely chopped
  green pepper
⅓ cup finely chopped
  onion
2 tbsp. butter
2 tbsp. all-purpose
  flour
2½ cups peeled, seeded
  and chopped fresh
  tomatoes

1 tsp. salt
1 cup grated Cheddar
  cheese
2 eggs, beaten
1 tsp. Worcestershire
  sauce
dash cayenne
  (optional)
hot toast

In skillet, sauté celery, green pepper and onion in butter, stirring frequently, until tender but not browned. Blend in flour. Add tomatoes and salt, and cook, stirring frequently over low heat until mixture thickens. Remove from heat. Add cheese and stir until it has melted. Slowly add a small amount of cheese mixture to beaten eggs and combine thoroughly. Return cheese-egg mixture to vegetables in skillet. Cook, over low heat, stirring constantly, for 2 to 3 minutes until thickened and creamy. Blend in Worcestershire sauce and cayenne. Serve piping hot over hot toast.

Cheese & Potato Pie

16 oz. cottage cheese
2 eggs, beaten
½ cup sour cream
2½ cups riced potatoes
1 tsp. salt

⅛ tsp. pepper
9" unbaked pie shell
  light cream
1 tbsp. butter
  paprika

Heat oven 375°F. Mix cheese, eggs, sour cream, potatoes, salt and pepper. Place into shell. Brush with cream, dot with butter and sprinkle with paprika. Bake 45 minutes. You can sprinkle diced bacon over top.

Muesli

1 unpeeled apple
1 banana
2 tbsp. raisins
½ cup rolled oats
2 tbsp. wheat germ

1 tsp. bran
½ cup yogurt
1 tbsp. chopped
    walnuts
4 almonds, chopped

Cube apple and banana into bowl. Sprinkle with raisins, oats, wheat germ and bran. Spoon yogurt over top. Sprinkle with chopped nuts. Makes 1 serving.

Energy Bars

3 cups granola or
    rolled oats
1 cup protein powder
    (vanilla or
    chocolate)

½ cup coconut
½ cup sunflower seeds
½ cup butter
1 cup peanut butter
½ cup honey

Mix dry ingredients in bowl. Melt butter and mix with honey and peanut butter. Add to dry ingredients. You can substitute raisins, nuts, dates, etc. Press in 8" x 8" Pyrex dish and cut into squares.

Super Granola

1 cup oil
1½ cups honey
5 cups oats
1 cup sliced almonds,
    or walnuts
1 cup sunflower seeds

1 cup coconut
½ cup wheat germ
½ cup soy flour
¼ cup bran
½ cup powdered milk
¼ cup sesame seeds

Warm honey and oil until thin. Combine everthing else and slowly pour liquids over. Blend thoroughly. Spread onto 2 cookie sheets. Bake at 250°F for 45 minutes, stirring every 5 minutes. Cool. Store in airtight container. Dried fruits such as raisins, dates, apricots may be added after baking.

Cottage Cheese Pancakes

2 cups creamed cottage
  cheese
⅔ cup fine dry bread
  crumbs
½ cup chopped green
  onion
2 tbsp. parsley

1 tsp. salt
¼ tsp. nutmeg
4 eggs
3 tbsp. butter or
  margarine
  Tomato-Mushroom
  sauce

Combine all ingredients, except butter and sauce. Beat with wooden spoon until well blended. Melt butter in large skillet. When butter begins to bubble drop in batter by ¼ cupfuls and cook until browned on both sides. Serve with Tomato-mushroom sauce. Makes about 16 pancakes.

Tomato-Mushroom Sauce

2 tbsp. olive oil
10 can mushrooms
   stems & pieces,
   drained
⅓ cup chopped green
   pepper

15 oz. can tomato sauce
   with tidbits
½ tsp. basil
¼ tsp. oregano
½ tsp. salt
⅛ tsp. pepper

Heat oil in skillet. Add mushrooms and green pepper, cook until barely tender. Add tomato sauce and seasonings. Simmer about 10 minutes.

An important marriage rule . . . a woman puts a little bit of sugar into everything she says to her man, and takes a little grain of salt with everything he says to her.

Soups

Potato Soup

4 cups diced potatoes
2 cups water
2 tbsp. salt
1 large onion, thinly
 sliced
6 cloves garlic, minced
1 tbsp. oil

3 cups milk
5 sprigs parsley,
 snipped
1 cup grated cheese
2 tbsp. butter
salt
pepper

Combine diced potatoes, water and salt and simmer until cooked. Sauté onion and garlic in oil. Add to potatoes along with milk, parsley, cheese, butter, salt and pepper to taste. Heat just to boiling point. Serve with croutons.

Oatmeal Vegetable Soup

3 qts. water
1 tbsp. salt
 potatoes, to make 2
 cups mashed
1 cup cream
1 cup butter
3 cups green beans,
 sliced ½" thick

1 cup carrots, sliced in
 thin rounds
1 cup diced celery
2 cups diced onions
6 cloves garlic, minced
2 cups oatmeal

Simmer potatoes for mashing in salt water. Take out and mash with ½ cup butter and ½ cup cream. Put aside. To water add all vegetables except onions and garlic. Sauté onions and garlic in ½ cup butter while other vegetables are simmering. Add oatmeal and onions to vegetables. Stir in mashed potatoes. Add rest of cream and bring to a boil. Add salt and pepper to taste.

"A woman is like a teabag. You never know her strength until she's in hot water."

Vegetable Broth

celery

onions

tomatoes

carrots

potatoes

turnip

cabbage

seasonings

Amounts and variety of vegetables may be varied as you wish. Chop vegetables and simmer in enough water, to cover all vegetables, for 2 hours. Add seasonings of your choice. Strain and use broth as a substitute for meat broths.

Barley Vegetable Soup

20 cups water

2 tbsp. salt

8 potatoes, quartered

½ cup barley

2 cups onions

6 cloves garlic

1 cup butter

6 cups canned
   tomatoes

1 cup butter

1 cup cream

1 cup chopped celery

1 cup sliced carrots

1 cup peas

1 cup corn

1 cup cut green beans

2 cups diced potatoes

Boil quartered potatoes and barley in salted water until tender. Sauté diced onion and garlic in ½ cup butter. Add tomatoes and simmer 15 minutes. Take cooked potatoes out and mash with ½ cup butter and 1 cup cream. To water add all remaining vegetables and simmer 5 minutes. Combine tomato and onion mixture with mashed potatoes and add all this to soup. Bring to boil, simmer another 5 minutes and remove. Add additional cream if you like a richer soup. Season with salt and pepper.

Lentil Soup

4 qts. water	1 cup diced celery
1 tbsp. salt	1 cup carrots
3 potatoes	1 cup butter
½ cup green split peas	2 cups diced onions
½ cup brown lentils	4 cloves garlic
½ cup red lentils	2 cups diced potatoes
	1½ cups whipping cream

Fill 6 quart pot ¾ full with hot water. Add 1 heaping tbsp. salt. Add 3 halved, peeled potatoes to water to make 1½ cups mashed. Add green split peas and lentils. Simmer along with potatoes until just about cooked, then add celery and carrots. Fry in 1 cup butter the onions and garlic. Prepare 2 cups diced potatoes. Take out boiled potatoes and mash with ½ cup butter and whipping cream. When other vegetables are just about cooked add diced potatoes and fried onions. Cook 5 minutes, add mashed potatoes. Season according to taste with salt and pepper. Sprinkle with diced green onions. Serve with croutons or crackers.

Manhattan Clam Chowder

3 slices diced bacon	1 cup diced potatoes
1 cup diced onions	2 cans clams
2 cups canned tomatoes	¼ tsp. thyme
1 cup diced carrots	1 cup cream (optional)
1 cup diced celery	

Fry bacon, add onions and sauté, then add tomatoes and simmer 10 minutes. To 2 quarts of boiling water, add carrots, celery, potatoes, clams plus all of the juice, and bacon-tomato mixture. Season with salt, pepper, and thyme. Serve with croutons.

Onion Soup

3 tbsp. butter
4 large onions, sliced
2 tbsp. flour
8 cups beef stock

salt and pepper
French bread, toasted
grated Parmesan
  cheese

Melt butter and cook onions until brown. Add flour and stir to blend. Stir in beef stock and simmer 10 minutes. Add salt and pepper to taste. Pour soup into individual oven-proof soup bowls. Top with toast and sprinkle toast thickly with Parmesan cheese. Put in oven and broil until cheese is nicely browned. Makes 6 to 8 servings.

Minestrone Soup

8 cups beef bouillon
  OR beef stock OR
  soy cube stock
1 cup dried yellow peas
3 tbsp. oil
1 cup chopped onion
2 cloves garlic, minced
1 cup canned tomatoes
1 cup chopped cabbage

1 cup chopped celery
1 cup chopped carrots
2 cups diced, cooked
  meat (optional)
½ cup uncooked
  macaroni
4 cups raw spinach,
  torn into pieces
grated Parmesan
  cheese
croutons

Heat bouillon to boiling in large pot. Add peas and simmer. Meanwhile heat oil in separate pan and sauté onion and garlic for 2 minutes. Add tomatoes and onion mixture to peas. Simmer 30 minutes. Add cabbage, celery, carrots and simmer 10 minutes. Add meat and macaroni and cook 5 minutes. Add spinach and continue simmering 5 more minutes. Serve immediately in soup bowls, sprinkle with Parmesan cheese and croutons.

Mushroom Soup

1 lb. fresh mushrooms,
   sliced
1 large onion, chopped
¼ cup butter
¼ cup flour
1 qt. chicken broth*

2 cups milk
1 cup cream
   salt and pepper to
   taste
¼ tsp. thyme
¼ tsp. cayenne

Sauté mushrooms and onion in butter. Add flour stirring to make a paste. Add 1 cup of the broth, stirring until slightly thickened; add remaining broth, milk, cream, salt, pepper and spices. Simmer another 5 minutes. Do not boil. *Note: chicken broth is optional, you may use water instead.

Asparagus Soup

1 lb. asparagus stocks
2 qts. water
1 cup butter
1 cup diced onions
2 cups diced asparagus
   tips
2 tbsp. flour
1 qt. milk
1 cup finely diced
   carrots, optional

1 cup diced celery,
   optional
2 cups finely diced
   potatoes, optional
1 cup cream
   salt & pepper to taste
   diced green onions
   croutons

Boil thick tough stocks of asparagus in water for ½ hour to make stock. Put through blender then sieve. Melt butter in pan. Sauté onion, asparagus, flour. Gradually add milk and start thickening, stirring frequently. Bring stock to a boil, add carrots, celery and potatoes, if wanted. Combine stock and sauce stirring contantly. Add cream, salt and pepper to taste, simmer 5 minutes. Sprinkle with green onions and serve with croutons.

1. Caesar Salad, Page 37
2. Chârtreuse of Vegetables, Page 46
3. Copper Penny Carrots, Page 41
4. Croutons, Page 44
5. Stuffed Baked Potatoes, Page 49
6. Zucchini Cutlets, Page 53

Creamy Broccoli Soup

2 tbsp. minced onion
3 tbsp. butter or
   margarine
3 tbsp. flour
   salt
3 cups milk
3 cups chicken broth
   (or 3 chicken
   bouillon cubes
   dissolved in 3 cups
   boiling water)

10 oz. pkg. frozen
   chopped broccoli,
   slightly thawed
2 cups thinly sliced
   carrots
pepper

In large saucepan sauté onion in butter until tender. With whisk stir in flour and 1½ tsps. salt; gradually add milk, stirring constantly, and bring to a boil. Add broth, broccoli and carrots. Cook over low heat (do not boil), stirring occasionally, about 25 minutes, or until carrots are tender and flavors blended. Add pepper and salt to taste. Serve hot. Makes 2 quarts.

Creamy Cauliflower Soup

1 medium head
   cauliflower, broken
   into buds
¼ cup chopped onion
4 tbsp. butter or
   margarine
¼ cup all-purpose flour

3 cups chicken broth
2 cups milk
1 tsp. Worcestershire
   sauce
1 cup sharp cheese,
   shredded
snipped chives

Cook cauliflower, covered, in small amount of boiling salted water for 10 to 15 minutes or until tender. Drain and coarsely chop. In large saucepan, cook onion in butter until tender but not brown. Blend in flour, add chicken broth, milk, and Worcestershire. Cook and stir until mixture thickens slightly; add cauliflower. Bring to boiling and stir in cheese. Sprinkle each serving with snipped chives. Makes 6 to 8 servings.

Carrot Chowder

3 cups diced carrots
1½ cups chopped onion
½ cup diced celery
3 tbsp. butter
2 cups diced raw
   potatoes
2 cups boiling water
2 chicken bouillon
   cubes

1½ tsp. salt
¼ tsp. pepper
½ cup chopped parsley
⅔ cup skim milk powder
2 cups cold water
½ cup grated Cheddar
   cheese

Sauté carrots, onion and celery in melted butter until onion is transparent, about 10 minutes. Add potatoes, boiling water and bouillon cubes. Stir until cubes dissolve. Add salt, pepper and parsley. Cover; simmer until vegetables are tender, about 15 minutes. Combine skim milk powder and cold water, or use 2½ cups of milk instead. Add to soup, and heat thoroughly. Serve sprinkled with grated cheese. Makes about 7 cups.

Cream of Carrot-Potato Soup

3 tbsp. butter
2 onions, finely
   chopped
1 clove garlic, minced
4 carrots, chopped
3 potatoes, peeled and
   diced
5 cups chicken broth

¼ tsp. pepper
½ tsp. thyme
1 bay leaf
   salt
¾ cup cream (optional)
   chopped green
   onions

In large saucepan, melt butter over medium heat. Cook onions and garlic until tender. Add carrots and potatoes, toss with onions. Add broth and seasonings, bring to boil. Reduce heat, cover, cook until vegetables are tender. Transfer soup to blender, and purée. Return to heat and add cream. Heat through. Sprinkle with green onions and serve. If you are using canned chicken broth or bouillon cubes, don't add too much salt!

24-Hour Salad

20½ oz. can pineapple
    tidbits (2½ cups)
3 egg yolks
2 tbsp. sugar
2 tbsp. vinegar
1 tbsp. butter

16 oz. can pitted light
    sweet cherries,
    drained
2 oranges, peeled,
    diced, and drained
2 cups miniature
    marshmallows
1 cup whipping cream

Drain pineapple, reserving 2 tbsp. syrup. In top of double boiler, beat egg yolks lightly; add the reserved pineapple syrup, sugar, vinegar, butter, and a dash of salt. Place over hot water; cook, stirring constantly, until mixture thickens slightly and barely coats a spoon, about 12 minutes. Cool to room temperature. Combine fruits and marshmallows. Pour custard over and mix gently. Whip cream; fold into fruit mixture. Turn into serving bowl. Cover and chill 24 hours. Garnish with fresh orange sections and mint leaves. Makes 6 to 8 servings.

Christmas Salad

3 oz. pkg. lime jelly
    powder
14 oz. can crushed
    pineapple
8 oz. pkg. cream
    cheese, softened

¼ cup chopped
    pimiento (optional)
1 cup diced celery
8 oz. evaporated milk,
    whipped
½ cup chopped nuts

Bring pineapple and juice to a boil. Dissolve jelly powder in this. Cool and add rest of ingredients. (Milk must be thoroughly chilled to whip.) Turn into ice-water-rinsed mold and refrigerate. Garnish with pimiento stars. Makes 6 to 8 servings.

Seven-Layer Salad

1 head lettuce,
  shredded
1 green pepper, diced
1 cup chopped celery
1 large onion, chopped
16 oz. can peas, drained

2 cups mayonnaise
2 tbsp. brown sugar
½ cup shredded
  Cheddar cheese
½ cup crisp bacon bits

In a large bowl layer ingredients one at a time in order given. Do not toss. Cover and refrigerate 8 hours or overnight. When ready dig deep for each layer and enjoy.

Caesar Salad

2 cloves garlic, minced
4 anchovy fillets
  (optional)
2 heads romaine
  lettuce
2 tomatoes, sliced
  (optional)
2 cucumbers, sliced
  (optional)
1 clove garlic
1 tsp. salt
½ tsp. dry mustard
½ tsp. freshly ground
  pepper

½ tsp. Worcestershire
  sauce
1 tbsp. lemon juice
2 tbsp. apple cider
  vinegar
½ cup olive or salad oil
1 raw egg
2 cups garlic salad
  croutons
½ cup grated Parmesan
  cheese

Rub garlic into serving bowl. Anchovy fillets may be mashed in with garlic. Tear lettuce into bite-sized pieces and put in bowl, along with tomatoes and cucumbers, if used. Blend well in blender, the next 9 ingredients.

Just before serving salad toss in croutons and Parmesan cheese. Toss with dressing and serve immediately. See photograph page 32.

Fresh Spinach Salad

8 cups torn spinach
3 hard-cooked eggs, grated
3 green onions, finely chopped

fresh mushrooms, sliced
½ cup cooked diced bacon, crumbled, or vega bits

Toss with dressing just before serving.

Dressing:

1 clove garlic
2 tbsp. cider or red wine vinegar
1 tsp. sugar

1 tsp. salt
1 tsp. dry mustard
½ tsp. lemon pepper
6 tbsp. oil

Blend in blender.

Coleslaw

Salad:

1 small head cabbage, shredded
2 medium onions, grated
2 carrots, shredded

2 stalks celery, chopped
1 head purple cabbage, shredded
2 cups cooked peas

Dressing:

¼ cup vinegar
¼ cup water
2 heaping tbsp. sugar
1 tsp. salt
1 tsp. prepared mustard

¼ cup salad oil
½ lemon juice
¼ cup sour cream
½ cup mayonnaise

Combine salad vegetables. Boil dressing mixture, except sour cream and mayonnaise. While still hot, pour over cabbage mixture and mix well. Add sour cream and mayonnaise, and chill. You may increase or decrease seasoning to suit your taste.

Vegetable Dill Combo

¼ cup creamy French
    salad dressing
¼ cup mayonnaise
2 tbsp. chili sauce
2 tsp. lemon juice
1¼ tsp. salt
1 tsp. dried dillweed
⅛ tsp. pepper
1½ cups diced carrot,
    cooked and
    drained

1½ cups cauliflower,
    sliced, cooked and
    drained
9 oz. pkg. frozen peas,
    cooked and
    drained
9 oz. pkg. frozen Italian
    green beans,
    cooked and
    drained
½ cup chopped celery
¼ cup chopped onion

Blend together French dressing, mayonnaise, chili sauce, lemon juice, salt, dillweed and pepper. Chill several hours or overnight. Arrange vegetables in large bowl. Add dressing; toss to coat. Makes 8 to 10 servings.

Vegetables Vinaigrette

⅔ cup salad oil
⅓ cup tarragon vinegar
    (or white)
1 tsp. sugar
1 tsp. salt
¼ tsp. Tabasco
1 tbsp. dill weed
2 tbsp. snipped parsley
1 tbsp. snipped chives

½-1 lb. fresh mushrooms,
    sliced
2 cups raw cauliflower
    buds
14 oz. can artichoke
    hearts, drained
14 oz. jar green beans,
    drained

Combine oil, vinegar, sugar, salt, Tabasco, dill, parsley and chives and mix until thoroughly blended. Pour over vegetables and marinate in refrigerator at least 3 hours before serving. This improves with age and keeps several days in refrigerator.

Kidney Bean Salad

28 oz. canned red kidney beans
4 cloves garlic
1 large onion, finely diced
½ cup finely diced celery
1 cup finely diced sweet pickles

8 hard-cooked eggs, chilled and diced
1 cup mayonnaise
salt and pepper to taste
½ tsp. paprika
½ cup diced green onions

Drain kidney beans well so no liquid remains. Mince garlic very fine and rub insides of 2-quart bowl. Dice very fine the onion, celery and sweet pickle and add to garlic along with beans and eggs. Add mayonnaise, salt and pepper to taste just before serving. Garnish with paprika and sprinkle with diced green onions. Makes 6 to 8 servings.

Greek Salad

Add vegetables in amounts you want:

sliced cucumber
thin onion rings
cherry tomatoes
green pepper chunks or strips

black olives
cauliflower
crumbled feta cheese

Dressing:

1 cup olive oil
½ cup white wine vinegar
½ tsp. dry mustard

1 tsp. sugar
2 cloves garlic, crushed
1 tsp. salt
dash pepper

Pour over vegetables. Marinate 1 hour. See photograph on cover.

Bulgar Salad

2 cups raw bulgar
2 cups hot water
1 tsp. salt
3 cloves garlic, minced
1½ cups raw sunflower
   seeds

½ cup lemon juice
½ cup oil
4 green onions, sliced
   parsley, snipped
   salt to taste
   dash cayenne

Put bulgar into hot water, let stand 2 hours or overnight. Cook until tender with the salt added. Mix in remaining ingredients and arrange on bed of lettuce.

Copper Penny Carrots

2 carrots, sliced in
   rounds
10 can oz. tomato soup
1 tsp. prepared
   mustard
1 tsp. Worcestershire
   sauce

½ cup oil
1 cup sugar
¾ cup vinegar
   salt and pepper
1 onion, thinly sliced
1 green pepper, sliced

Cook sliced carrots in salted water until still crisp, drain, cool. In saucepan boil next 8 ingredients. In dish layer carrots, onions and pepper. Pour cooled sauce over, let stand overnight. See photograph page 32.

Super Macaroni Salad

5 cups cold cooked
   macaroni
2 cups chopped sweet
   pickles
6 cloves garlic, minced

1 cup diced onion
1 cup diced celery
1 cup finely diced
   Cheddar cheese
1 cup mayonnaise (or
   more)

Combine everything, then mix in mayonnaise to taste. Add salt and pepper to taste.

Potato Salad

2 lbs. potatoes, boiled and diced	1 green pepper, finely diced
1 cup finely chopped celery	9 hard-cooked eggs salt and pepper to taste
1 cup finely chopped onion	1 cup mayonnaise
1 cucumber, finely diced	1 tbsp. dry mustard
	1 tbsp. sour cream

Finely chop 6 eggs and 2 whites, and put in bowl with all the vegetables. Mix a dressing of the mayonnaise, mustard, sour cream and 2 egg yolks, mashed. Toss dressing with vegetables. Slice last egg and use for decoration.

Herb Dressing

2 hard-cooked eggs	½ tsp. dry mustard
1 raw egg yolk	1½ tsp. lemon juice OR vinegar
½ cup olive oil	
1 tbsp. minced mixed herbs (parsley, oregano, chives, thyme)	½ tsp. salt
	¼ tsp. pepper

Chop egg whites. Mash yolks and beat with raw yolk. Add oil a few drops at a time. Add everything else except whites. Beat well. Add finely chopped whites. Makes ¾ cup dressing.

Thousand Island Dressing

1 cup salad dressing	2 tbsp. olives with pimiento
¼ cup chili sauce	
2 tbsp. green pepper, finely diced	1 hard-cooked egg, grated

Mix together and chill.

Thousand Island Dressing

1 qt. French dressing
1 qt. mayonnaise
1 green pepper
2 stalks celery

1 tbsp. horseradish
2 green onions
4 oz. pimiento

Blend everything in blender.

French Dressing

10 oz. can condensed
    tomato soup
½ cup brown sugar
¾ cup vinegar
1 cup oil

2 tsp. paprika
2 cloves garlic
1 small onion
1 tsp. salt

Blend everything in blender.

Roquefort Dressing

4 oz. blue cheese
¼ cup milk
1 tsp. garlic, minced
1 tsp. onion salt
1 tsp. paprika

1 tbsp. sugar
⅛ tsp. Tabasco
1 tsp. H. P. Sauce
2 cups mayonnaise
buttermilk

Mix all ingredients and thin with buttermilk, if needed.

Buttermilk Coleslaw Dressing

½ cup buttermilk
½ cup mayonnaise
1 tbsp. vinegar
½ tsp. Worcestershire

½ tsp. salt
½ tsp. pepper
1 tsp. sugar
dash of paprika

Blend ingredients well in order given. Chill.

Green Goddess Dressing

1 cup snipped parsley
½ cup chopped chives
1 cup sour cream
1 cup mayonnaise
2 tbsp. sugar
2 tbsp. anchovy paste

1 tsp. salt
1 tsp. pepper
¼ tsp. garlic
½ cup wine vinegar
½ cup red wine
1 tsp. tarragon

Blend in blender.

Italian Dressing

¼ cup vinegar
½ tsp. sugar
½ tsp. dry mustard
¼ tsp. garlic powder
¾ cup oil
1 tsp. Worcestershire
   sauce
1 tbsp. water

¼ tsp. onion powder
¼ tsp. pepper
1 tbsp. lemon juice
¼ tsp. oregano
½ tsp. salt
¼ tsp. sweet red pepper
   flakes

Combine everything except oil. Shake well. Add oil and shake until creamy. Makes 1 cup.

Garlic Butter or Croutons

½ cup soft butter
½ cup oil
1 tsp. salt
1 tsp. garlic powder

3 cloves garlic
any other spices you
   like, thyme,
   parsley, etc.

Blend well in blender. Spread very thinly on bread slicees. Slice bread into tiny ¼" cubes. Bake 300°F ½ hour or so stirring them every 5 minutes. For bacon flavor use leftover bacon fat instead of oil. Adjust spices to taste. This mixture may also be used as garlic butter for garlic bread. See photograph page 32.

Chartreuse of Vegetables

½ lb. fresh whole green beans
½ lb. fresh carrots sliced into sticks
1 zucchini sliced into ¼" circles
10 oz. frozen peas

½ lb. broccoli florets
½ lb. cauliflower florets
12 Brussels sprouts
¾ cup butter
4 cups well-seasoned, thick-mashed potatoes

Preheat oven to 350°F. Parboil vegetables separately and let cool. If using frozen green beans, season with salt, pepper and garlic powder. Line a 1½-quart flat-bottomed casserole pan with all of the butter. Make a thick layer on bottom and sides. This will hold the vegetables in place. Line bottom edge with peas pressed into butter to stay in place. Fill center with overlapping zucchini slices on bottom of casserole in a circle between peas to make a flowery design. Alternate green beans and carrot sticks by standing them along the side of casserole and pressing them to make them stick to the sides in butter. Then line bottom and sides of casserole with a layer of mashed potatoes leaving a well in the middle. Fill with cauliflower, broccoli and Brussels sprouts. Pack the casserole well with remaining mashed potatoes just up to carrots and beans. Place casserole on a shallow pan as the butter will bubble in oven. Bake 350°F for 30 minutes. To serve put a platter over top and turn casserole over to release the vegetable chartreuse. See photograph page 32.

Breaded Cauliflower

1 large head cauliflower
2 eggs, well beaten salad oil

1 cup bread crumbs, seasoned with salt and pepper (OR cracker OR corn-flake crumbs)

Wash and separate cauliflower into florets. Cook in salted water 12 to 15 minutes. Do not overcook. They must be firm enough to handle. Drain. Dip florets into egg, then roll in crumbs. Fry in hot salad oil until golden brown and tender.

Broccoli Casserole

1½ lbs. fresh broccoli,
  cut up (6 cups)
10 oz. can condensed
  cream of
  mushroom soup
¼ cup mayonnaise, or
  salad dressing

¼ cup shredded sharp
  cheese
1 tbsp. chopped
  pimiento (optional)
1½ tsp. lemon juice
⅓ cup rich round
  cheese cracker
  crumbs

In covered saucepan, cook broccoli in small amount of boiling salted water for 10 to 15 minutes; drain. Turn into 1½-quart casserole. Combine soup, mayonnaise, cheese, pimiento, and lemon juice. Pour over broccoli. Top with cracker crumbs. Bake in 350°F oven for 35 minutes. Makes 6 to 8 servings.

Spinach-Stuffed Onions

10 oz. pkg. frozen
  chopped spinach
3 oz. pkg. cream
  cheese, softened
1 egg
½ cup soft bread
  crumbs

¼ cup grated Parmesan
  cheese
¼ cup milk
¼ tsp. salt
  dash pepper
1 large flat white onion

Cook spinach according to package directions; drain well and set aside. Beat together cream cheese and egg until light. Add crumbs, Parmesan, milk, salt and pepper; mix well. Stir in drained spinach. Peel onion and cut in half crosswise. Separate layers to form shells; place in a 9" x 9" x 2" baking dish. Fill in base of shells with smaller onion pieces, if necessary. Spoon spinach mixture into shells. Cover baking dish with foil. Bake in 350°F oven for 35 to 40 minutes or until onion shells are tender and filling is set. Makes about 6 servings.

Potatoes For Stuffing

baking potatoes (long   melted butter
thin ones are best)

Heat oven to 400°F. Scrub potatoes very well and prick each in a few places on 1 side only. Put on baking sheet and bake about 1 hour or until fork tender. Cut a thin slice from sides of potatoes where they are pricked. Discard slices. Carefully scoop pulp out of potatoes into a bowl leaving about ¼" of potato inside the skins to make shells to hold fillings. Set these shells back on baking sheet and brush all over inside with melted butter. Return to oven for about 7 minutes to crisp.

Spinach-Cheese Potatoes

6 large baking potatoes   ⅓ cup light cream
3 tbsp. butter   ¾ cup grated Swiss
2 tbsp. flour   cheese
½ tsp. salt   1 cup cooked spinach
¼ tsp. pepper   OR peas
1½ cups milk   2 tbsp. fine dry bread
                                    crumbs

Prepare potatoes as directed in Potatoes For Stuffing above, and leave oven set at 400°F. Melt butter in saucepan. Stir in flour, salt and pepper and let bubble up. Remove from heat and add milk and cream, all at once. Stir to blend. Return to moderate heat and cook, stirring constantly, until thickened and smooth. Add cheese and heat, stirring, just until cheese is melted. Measure out ½ cup of this cheese sauce and blend it with the cooked spinach. Keep remaining cheese sauce warm to serve over potatoes. Beat hot potato pulp with electric mixer until smooth and fluffy. Blend in spinach mixture. Spoon into crisp potato shells and set on baking sheet. Sprinkle each potato with 1 tsp. bread crumbs. Bake 15 to 20 minutes.

Stuffed Baked Potatoes

6 large baking potatoes
¼ cup hot milk
¼ cup heavy cream, warmed
2 tbsp. soft butter
1 tsp. salt
¼ tsp. pepper
¼ tsp. garlic salt
melted butter
¼ cup grated Swiss cheese

Prepare potatoes as directed in Potatoes For Stuffing page 48 and leave oven set at 400°F after potatoes are baked. Beat hot potato pulp, milk, cream, 2 tbsp. butter, salt, pepper and garlic salt with electric mixer until smooth and fluffy. Spoon into crisped potato shells and set on baking sheet. Brush tops of potatoes lightly with melted butter and sprinkle with grated cheese. Bake 15 to 20 minutes or until lightly browned and very hot. Serves 6. See photograph page 32.

Potato Nests

6 medium potatoes
1 cup diced onion
½ cup butter
2 OR 3 eggs, lightly beaten
seasoned bread crumbs
1 tbsp. cooked peas
1 tbsp. fresh cream
cayenne OR paprika
thin cheese strips

Boil potatoes; mash and add onion, butter, eggs. Roll in crushed seasoned bread crumbs the size of 1" balls. Put on greased cookie sheet. Shape like birds' nests with hole in center. Add peas and cream. Sprinkle cayenne or paprika on top. Bake 400°F for 20 minutes. Prepare thin cheese strips and put across to melt.

A good listener is not only popular everywhere, but after a while he knows something.

Carrots au Gratin

¼ cup plus 3 tbsp. butter
¼ cup finely chopped onion
¼ cup all-purpose flour
1½ cups milk
⅓ cup grated Cheddar cheese
1 tbsp. finely chopped parsley
⅛ to ¼ tsp. salt
pepper
2 cups cooked, thinly sliced carrots
2 cups cornflakes, crushed into fine crumbs

Melt ¼ cup butter in a saucepan; add onion and cook over low heat, stirring frequently, until onion is soft. Stir in flour and blend well. Remove saucepan from heat and add milk slowly, stirring constantly. Cook milk mixture over low heat, stirring continually, until thickened and smooth. Remove from heat. Add cheese, parsley, salt and a pinch of pepper. Stir until cheese melts. Add cooked carrots. Turn into buttered 1-quart casserole. Melt remaining 3 tbsps. butter in a saucepan. Remove saucepan from heat and add cornflake crumbs to melted butter. Toss lightly. Top carrot mixture with cornflake crumbs. Bake 375°F for about 20 minutes. Garnish with parsley and serve at once. Makes 4 servings.

Eggplant Patties

1 medium eggplant, pared and cubed
1½ cups cracker crumbs
1½ cups shredded sharp cheese
2 eggs, lightly beaten
2 tbsp. snipped parsley
2 tbsp. sliced green onion
1 clove garlic, minced
½ tsp. salt
⅛ tsp. pepper
2 tbsp. cooking oil

In covered saucepan, cook eggplant in boiling water until tender, about 5 minutes. Drain very well and mash. Stir in crumbs, cheese, eggs, parsley, onion, garlic, salt, and pepper. Shape into 8 patties about 3" in diameter. Cook in hot oil about 3 minutes on each side until golden brown. Makes 4 servings.

Cheese-Nut Loaf

4 eggs, beaten
1 lb. Cheddar cheese,
    coarsely shredded
1½ cups finely chopped
    walnuts
1 cup cooked brown
    rice
½ cup quick-cooking
    rolled oats

½ cup finely chopped
    fresh mushrooms
1 medium onion,
    minced
1 clove garlic, minced
¼ tsp. salt
⅛ tsp. pepper
1 recipe Mushroom
    Sauce

Combine all ingredients except Mushroom Sauce in large bowl and mix well. Pack firmly into well-greased 9" x 5" x 3" loaf pan lined with greased waxed paper. Bake in 350°F oven for 50 minutes, or until firm. Let stand 10 minutes. Turn out on warm serving dish. Cut in slices and serve with Mushroom Sauce below.

Mushroom Sauce:

⅓ cup butter
½ lb. mushrooms,
    sliced (2 cups)
3 tbsp. flour

½ tsp. salt
dash of cayenne
2 cups milk

Melt butter in saucepan. Add mushrooms and cook and stir about 5 minutes, or until golden. Stir in flour, salt and cayenne. Gradually stir in milk and cook, stirring until thickened. Makes 6 to 8 servings.

Walnut Burgers

1 cup grated cheese
1 cup walnuts, ground
1 cup crumbs
½ tsp. sage

pepper to taste
1 onion, diced
1 tsp. salt
5 eggs, beaten

Mix together. Fry like patties. Serve with tomato sauce.

Curried Asparagus Sticks

1 lb. fresh asparagus
   spears
1 egg
2 tbsp. water
½ tsp. curry powder
   dash salt

dash white pepper
1 cup fine dry bread
   crumbs
3 tbsp. butter
4 green pepper rings

In skillet, lay asparagus spears flat. Cook, covered, in small amount of boiling salted water just until tender, about 10 minutes, drain. Beat together egg, water, curry, salt and pepper. Roll asparagus spears in crumbs; dip in egg mixture and roll again in crumbs. Brown slowly in same skillet in butter for 5 to 8 minutes, turning occasionally. To serve, make 4 bundles by inserting cooked spears through pepper rings. Makes 4 servings.

Italian Zucchini Pie

4 cups thinly sliced
   zucchini
1 cup chopped onion
½ cup butter
½ cup snipped parsley
½ tsp. salt
½ tsp. pepper
¼ tsp. garlic powder
¼ tsp. basil

¼ tsp. oregano
2 eggs, well beaten
2 cups grated
   mozzarella cheese
235 g can Pillsbury
   crescent dinner
   rolls
2 tsp. prepared
   mustard OR Dijon

Heat oven to 375°F. Fry onion and zucchini in butter for 10 minutes. Stir in parsley and seasonings. In bowl blend eggs and cheese. Stir in vegetable mixture. Separate rolls and place in ungreased 11" quiche or pie pan. Spread crust with mustard. Pour in vegetables. Bake 20 minutes. Let stand 10 minutes before cutting.

Zucchini Cutlets

½ cup chopped white
    and green onions
½ cup grated carrots
½ cup chopped green
    and red pepper
1 clove garlic, diced
2 cups finely ground
    soda crackers

2 heaping tbsp. flour
1 tsp. baking powder
¾ tsp. salt
⅛ tsp. pepper
3 cups shredded
    zucchini
2 eggs

Combine all ingredients, add eggs last. Heat ¼ cup of oil in frying pan. Drop mixture by large spoonfuls, into hot oil, shape into patties. Fry both sides. See photograph page 32.

Meatless Sausages

3 cups mashed cooked
    dried beans
⅔ cup bread crumbs
2 eggs

2 tbsp. Crisco
½ tsp. each salt, pepper
    and sage
2 eggs, beaten
1 cup seasoned crumbs

Mix everything, shape into sausages and dip into beaten egg, then crumbs. Fry in oil.

Meatless Patties

2 pkg. yeast
½ cup warm water
1 tsp. sugar
3 cups oats
2 cups wheat germ
2 onions, diced
2½ tsp. salt

4 eggs, beaten
1 tbsp. sage
½ cup finely chopped
    walnuts OR ground
1 tbsp. garlic salt
28 oz. canned milk

Dissolve sugar in warm water, sprinkle on yeast. Let stand 10 minutes, stir to dissolve. Combine all ingredients and make patties. Fry in ¼ cup of oil. Serve with tomato sauce.

Meatless "Meatballs"

2 boiled eggs, diced
¾ cup onion, diced
1 cup celery, diced
½ cup bread crumbs
½ cup cheese, shredded
1 cup wheat germ

¼ cup melted butter
2 cloves garlic, minced
1 tbsp. parsley, chopped
1 tsp. salt
pepper to taste
2 beaten eggs

Combine everything, add beaten eggs last. Shape into small meatballs or tiny patties. Fry in oil or bake in greased pan 325°F for 1 hour, covered. Serve with spaghetti and sauce. See photograph on cover.

Vegetable Crepes

3 tbsp. olive oil
¾ cup onion, chopped
¾ cup scallions, chopped
2 cloves garlic, minced
1½ cups diced green pepper
2 cups peeled and diced tomatoes
1 tsp. crushed basil

2 tsp. crushed parsley
salt and pepper
⅓ cup milk
⅓ cup flour
2 eggs
1 tbsp. butter, melted
3 oz. grated Swiss or Gruyère cheese
2 oz. grated Parmesan cheese

Heat olive oil in large skillet, sauté onion, scallions, garlic and green pepper until onion is transparent. Add tomatoes and increase the heat. Stir in herbs, season liberally with salt and pepper, continue cooking and stirring until water from tomatoes is nearly evaporated. Correct seasonings, remove from heat. Blend together all ingredients for the batter: milk, flour, eggs, butter and a little salt. Put batter aside for ½ hour. When vegetable mixture has cooled, stir in batter. Melt some butter in a heavy-bottomed skillet and pour out a little less than ¼ cup of batter for each crêpe. Fry to a golden brown on both sides. Arrange crepes on cookie sheets, sprinkle a heaping tablespoon of the cheeses on each one. If they have been allowed to cool, place crêpes in a 350°F for 7 or 8 minutes. Serves 4 to 5.

Mushroom Crepes

1¼ cups flour	5 eggs
1½ tbsp. sugar	1½ cups milk
¾ tsp. salt	1½ tbsp. melted butter

Measure flour, sugar and salt into sifter. Beat eggs. Sift in flour mixture and beat until smooth. Stir in milk and melted butter. Pour by a tbsp. into a preheated small crêpe pan and cook a minute on each side. Place crêpe on a buttered plate and add a tbsp. of filling (see below). Roll like jelly-roll. Place in greased Pyrex pan. Do not crowd crêpes. Pour tomato sauce over crêpes (see below). Cover with foil and bake in a preheated oven at 350°F for 20 minutes. (Crêpes can be frozen without sauce.)

Crêpe Filling:

2 cups diced onions	½ cup fine dry bread crumbs
⅓ lb. butter	salt and pepper to taste
2 cups drained sliced mushrooms	
4 cups diced, bread cubes	

Lightly fry onions in butter. Add mushrooms. When slightly golden, add bread and bread crumbs. Let mixture absorb butter. Take off stove and add salt and pepper to taste.

Tomato Sauce:

¼ lb. butter	salt and pepper to taste
1 cup diced onions	½ cup whipping cream
6 cloves garlic, minced	
1 qt. canned tomatoes	

Fry onions and garlic in butter. Add tomatoes and salt and pepper to taste. Simmer for about ½ hour. Add whipping cream and remove from stove.

Cabbage Pie

3 cups flour
2 tsp. baking powder
1 tsp. salt
1 cup margarine

¾ cup buttermilk OR
   sour cream
1 egg

Sift dry ingredients, add margarine and work into fine crumbs. Add egg to buttermilk, beat lightly and stir into the flour mixture. Knead lightly. Divide into portions large enough to fit pie plate. Roll fairly thin, fit into pie plate and fill with Cabbage Filling (below). Roll out more dough and place on top of filling for a top crust. Brush with cream or canned milk and bake at 350°F for 25 to 30 minutes. Remove from oven and cover with double thickness tea towel. Pies can be eaten hot, warm or cold. They freeze very well. The filling recipe is enough for 4, 9" pies.

Cabbage Filling:

½ cup Mazola oil
2 large onions, finely
   diced
2 10 oz. cans sliced
   mushrooms,
   drained

16 cups shredded
   cabbage
1 qt. canned tomatoes
   salt and pepper to
   taste
⅛ tsp. cayenne

Into large pot put oil, onion and mushrooms. Fry until glossy and add cabbage. Fry for a few minutes, then add tomatoes, salt, pepper and cayenne. Cook, stirring frequently till there is only a little juice left. Fill the pie shell.

"You can stay young forever, if you eat and drink moderately, get lots of sleep, exercise daily and lie about your age."

Maryland Fried Chicken

4-6 lb. frying chicken, cut
   in pieces
²⁄₃ cup flour
2 eggs
½ cup milk
2 cups fine dry bread
   crumbs
½ combination of
½ cup shortening and
   cup butter

1 tbsp. salt
¼ tsp. pepper
½ tsp. poultry
   seasoning
1 cup fresh cream
2 large onions, thinly
   sliced

Pat chicken dry and dip first into flour, coating well, then into egg which has been beaten slightly and diluted with the milk, then into crumbs. Coat well and shake off excess. Preheat frying pan to 360°F, add fat. Brown chicken without overcrowding, turn to brown all sides. Remove browned pieces to a pie pan. Scrape out breading particles and add more shortening before browning next batch. When all pieces are browned, place chicken in frying pan, sprinkle evenly with salt, pepper and poultry seasoning. Add cream and scatter onions over chicken. Cover, open vent, reduce heat to 220°F. Simmer until chicken is very tender, about 60 minutes. Remove chicken to heated platter.

Cream Gravy:

drippings
1 lb. mushrooms
⅓ cup flour
½ tsp. salt
⅛ tsp. pepper
¼ tsp. paprika

3 to 3½ cups milk (OR
   use ½ chicken
   broth)
1 tbsp. finely chopped
   parsley
sherry (optional)

Set dial at 360°F and boil down any remaining juices until only drippings remain. Fry mushrooms in drippings. Blend flour with drippings, stirring until well mixed and browned. Add salt, pepper, paprika and slowly add 3 to 3½ cups milk, or milk and broth, according to desired thickenss. Cook, stirring, until thickened. Add parsley and sherry to taste, if used. Serve with chicken.

Lemon-Baked Chicken

⅔ cup lemon juice
⅔ cup water
½ cup ketchup
3 tbsp. dark brown sugar
3 tbsp. paprika
3 tbsp. onion powder
1 tbsp. garlic powder

1 tbsp. cornstarch
1 tsp. dry mustard
¾ tsp. ground red pepper
4 tbsp. salad oil
6 lbs. chicken pieces
lemon slices

Preheat oven to 350°F. In a small saucepan, combine all but oil, chicken and lemon slices; blend well. Stir in salad oil. Cook, stirring constantly for 3 minutes until mixture thickens. Remove from heat and set aside. Place chicken in a 13" x 9" x 2" baking pan; brush with sauce. Bake about 1 hour, turning and brushing with sauce occasionally, or until chicken is tender. Garnish with lemon slices.

Chili Con Carne

6 cloves garlic, minced
1 cup diced onions
1 tbsp. butter
2 lbs. ground beef
1 cup ketchup
½ cup water
1 cup diced celery
1 green pepper, chopped
½ cup carrots, chopped
2 tbsp. lemon juice
1 tbsp. brown sugar
2 tsp. Worcestershire sauce

1 tbsp. vinegar
1 tsp. dry mustard
4 cups cooked kidney beans
1 tsp. chili powder
2 10 oz. cans sliced mushrooms
1 cup barbecue sauce
dash cayenne
salt and pepper to taste
2 tbsp. molasses
1 tsp. garlic powder

Brown the garlic and onions in butter. Add meat and fry until just browned. Drain off excess fat. Add everything else and simmer slowly 1 to 2 hours, stirring occasionally. Serve with garlic bread. See photograph page 64.

Rib Roast Barbecue

½ cup Burgundy
½ cup vinegar
½ cup cooking oil
¼ cup finely chopped
   onion
2 tbsp. sugar
1 tbsp. Worcestershire
1½ tsp. salt

½ tsp. pepper
½ tsp. dry mustard
¼ tsp. chili powder
⅛ tsp. dried thyme
1 clove garlic, minced
5 drops Tabasco
5 to 6 lb. rolled rib
   roast

Combine all ingredients except roast. Marinate roast 3 hours at room temperature or overnight in refrigerator. Drain, reserving marinade. Insert spit through center of roast, adjust holding forks. Insert meat thermometer. (Have medium coals at rear of firebox and a drip pan under meat). Lower hood; roast 2½ to 3 hours for medium-rare. Brush with marinade during last ½ hour. 140°F for rare, 160°F for medium, 170°F for well done. Let stand 15 minutes before carving.

Meat Loaf Roll

10 oz. fresh broccoli,
   chopped
2 lbs. ground beef
2 eggs
¾ cup soft bread
   crumbs
¼ cup ketchup
¼ cup milk

½ tsp. salt
¼ tsp. pepper
¼ tsp. oregano
1 tsp. salt
4 slices smoked ham
3 slices mozzarella
   cheese, 3" x 3",
   halved diagonally

Cook broccoli. Mix next 8 ingredients. Pat mixture into rectangle 12" x 10" on aluminum foil 18" x 15". Top with broccoli to within ½" of edges. Sprinkle with salt. Top with ham. Roll up rectangle beginning at 10" side, using foil to lift. Seal edges and ends of roll. Place on rack in shallow pan. Cook uncovered at 350°F 1¼ hours. Overlap cheese on top; cook until cheese melts, about 1 minute. To do ahead roll, cover and refrigerate meat loaf, no longer than 24 hours. Cook 1½ hours. See photograph page 64.

Beef en Brochette

½ cup red wine
¼ cup oil
½ cup brown sugar
¼ cup vinegar
1 tbsp. parsley flakes
⅛ tsp. pepper
dash each of garlic and onion powders and salt

1 lb. boneless chuck, cut in 1" cubes
½ cup mushrooms, halved
2 small onions, quartered
1 green pepper, in 2" chunks
1 tomato, in eighths
14 oz. can pineapple chunks, drained (optional)

Mix wine, oil, sugar, vinegar and seasonings in large bowl. Add beef, mushrooms, onions, green pepper, tomato and pineapple, mix well. Cover and refrigerate several hours or overnight. Thread meat and vegetables on skewers, broil about 5" from heat 15 to 20 minutes, turning once. See photograph page 64.

Ground Beef Stroganoff

½ cup chopped onion
2 tbsp. fat
1 lb. ground beef
2 tbsp. flour
1 tsp. salt
¼ tsp. pepper
1 clove garlic, crushed

10 oz. can sliced mushrooms, drained
10 oz. can condensed cream of mushroom soup
1 cup dairy sour cream
3 cups cooked noodles

Sauté onion in fat until transparent. Add beef and brown. Drain off excess fat. Stir in flour, salt, pepper and garlic. Add mushrooms and soup; bring to boil. Reduce heat and simmer uncovered for 10 minutes. Stir in sour cream and heat thoroughly, but do not boil. Serve over noodles. Serves 6.

Country-Style Stroganoff

1½ lbs. round or
    boneless chuck
    steak
2 tbsp. flour
1 tsp. salt
1 tsp. pepper
¼ cup shortening

1½ cups sliced onion
½ lb. sliced mushrooms
1½ cups stewed
    tomatoes
1 tsp. Worcestershire
    sauce
1 cup sour cream

Slice steak into ¼" slices. Coat with flour, salt and pepper. Melt shortening and fry meat until brown. Add onions and mushrooms. Cook 3 minutes. Add tomatoes and Worcestershire. Simmer until tomatoes thicken. Add sour cream and simmer ½ hour. Serve on top of cooked noodles.

Schnitzel

6 pork loin cutlets (1½
    lbs.) ½" thick
¼ cup flour
1 tsp. seasoned salt
¼ tsp. pepper
1 beaten egg
2 tbsp. milk
¾ cup fine dry bread
    crumbs

1 tsp. paprika
3 tbsp. shortening
¾ cup chicken broth
1 tbsp. flour
¼ tsp. dried dillweed
½ cup sour cream

Pound pork to ¼" to ½" thickness. Cut small slits around edges to prevent curling. Coat meat with mixture of the ¼ cup flour, the seasoned salt, and pepper. Combine egg and milk. Dip cutlets in egg mixture, then in mixture of crumbs and paprika. In large skillet, cook 3 cutlets at a time in hot shortening 2 to 3 minutes on each side. Remove from pan to platter; keep warm. Pour broth into skillet, scraping to loosen crusty drippings. Blend the 1 tbsp. flour and dillweed into sour cream. Stir sour cream mixture into broth. Cook and stir until mixture is thickened; but do not boil. Pass sauce with cutlets. Makes 6 servings.

Barbecued Pork Chops

6 pork chops
2 tbsp. flour
½ tsp. salt
½ cup shortening
1 large onion, chopped
1 green pepper,
  chopped
2 tbsp. brown sugar

2 tbsp. lemon juice
2 tsp. Worcestershire
  sauce
1 tsp. chili powder
½ tsp. salt
½ tsp. prepared
  mustard
1 can tomato sauce
1 cup water

Shake chops in flour and salt, and brown in shortening. Sauté onions and peppers with chops. Add rest of ingredients, stir together and return chops to pan. Bake 60 minutes at 350°F. Serve sauce poured over chops. See photograph page 64.

Oven-Barbecued Ribs

4 lbs. pork spareribs,
  cut in serving-size
  pieces
1 tbsp. butter
1 clove garlic, minced
½ cup ketchup
⅓ cup chili sauce
2 tbsp. brown sugar

2 tbsp. chopped onion
1 tbsp. prepared
  mustard
1 tbsp. Worcestershire
  sauce
1 tsp. celery seed
¼ tsp. salt
⅛ tsp. Tabasco
3 thin lemon slices

In large saucepan, add enough salted water to ribs to cover. Cover pan and simmer until nearly tender, about 1 hour. Meanwhile in saucepan, melt butter, add garlic and cook 4 to 5 minutes. Add ketchup, chili sauce, brown sugar, onion, mustard, Worcestershire, celery seed, salt, hot pepper sauce, and lemon slices. Bring to a boil. Drain ribs, place in shallow baking pan, and pour boiling sauce over ribs. Bake in 350°F oven for 30 minutes, basting often with sauce. Makes 4 servings.

Chef's Secret Meat Sauce

1 cup mayonnaise
⅓ cup chili sauce
¼ cup prepared
   mustard
¼ cup shredded onion

1 tbsp. horseradish
1 tsp. leaf oregano
⅛ tsp. cayenne pepper
⅓ cup dairy sour cream

Mix first 7 ingredients in bowl. Beat with a fork to mix thoroughly. Blend in sour cream. Let stand in refrigerator for several hours to mellow. Keeps well, refrigerated, for several days. Serve with hot or cold meats, poultry or fish.

Big Mac

1½ lbs. hamburger
⅓ can beef broth

1 jar veal OR liver baby
   food
1 tsp. salt and pepper

Combine everything. Shape into patties and fry.

Big Mac Dressing:

⅓ cup French dressing
1 cup salad dressing
1 tbsp. sugar
1 tsp. salt

¼ tsp. pepper
¼ cup sweet pickle,
   diced
1 tsp. onion powder

Combine all ingredients. Spread onto hamburger buns.

Baked Salmon

1 salmon
2 large onions, sliced

1 cup mayonnaise
1 pkg. onion soup mix

In 9" x 12" x 2" pan or according to size of fish, set fish on a layer of sliced onions. Split salmon in half, skin side up, and spread skin with mayonnaise. Sprinkle onion soup mix over top. Cover with foil. Bake 350°F 30 minutes or more according to fish size.

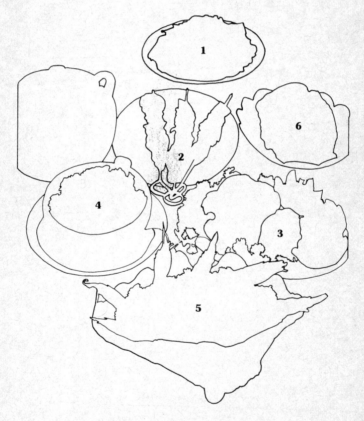

1. Barbecued Pork Chops, Page 63
2. Beef En Brochette, Page 61
3. Chicken Saltimbocca, Page 88
4. Chili Con Carne, Page 59
5. Cod Thermidor, Page 65
6. Meat Loaf Roll, Page 60

Seafood Newburg

⅓ cup butter
2 tbsp. enriched flour
2 cups light cream
4 egg yolks, lightly
  beaten

2 cups seafood, cooked
  or canned
½ tsp. salt
¼ cup cooking sherry
2 tsp. lemon juice

In top of double boiler, melt butter in saucepan, blend in flour, and gradually stir in cream. Cook slowly, stir constantly until thick. Place pan over hot water. Stir small amounts of sauce into egg yolks, return to pan and cook until blended, stirring constantly about 1 minute. Add seafood of your choice and salt. Heat thoroughly. Add sherry and lemon juice. Sprinkle with paprika. Makes 5 to 6 servings.

Cod Thermidor

1 lb. fresh or frozen
  cod fillets
1 small onion,
  quartered
  lemon slice
10 oz. can cream of
  mushroom soup
4 oz. can undrained
  shrimp
3 tbsp. flour
¼ cup milk

¼ cup dry white wine
¼ cup (1 oz.) shredded
  mozzarella cheese
2 tbsp. snipped parsley
½ cup soft bread
  crumbs
2 tbsp. grated
  Parmesan cheese
2 tsp. butter, melted
½ tsp. paprika

Thaw fish, skin and bone if necessary. Cut in ½" cubes. Place fish, onion, and lemon in greased skillet. Add water to cover. Bring to boil, simmer, covered, 5 to 6 minutes, until fish flakes easily. In a small saucepan, blend soup, shrimp and flour, gradually stir in milk and wine. Cook and stir until thickened. Stir in mozzarella and parsley. Heat through. Drain fish well and fold into sauce. Spoon into 4 coquille shells. Combine crumbs, Parmesan, butter and paprika. Sprinkle over sauce. Broil 1 to 2 minutes. Makes 4 servings. See photograph page 64.

Salmonettes Heloise

15 oz. can pink salmon
1 egg

1 heaping tsp. baking
   powder
½ cup flour

Drain the juice from salmon into a measuring cup and set aside. Put the drained salmon in a mixing bowl with the egg. Use fork to break up salmon and mix in the egg very well. Add ½ cup of sifted flour. Stir in flour thoroughly with fork again. This mixture will be very thick. Do not add any salt. Add pepper if desired. Take ¼ cup of the salmon juice, add 1 heaping teaspoon of baking powder to the juice and beat with a fork. It will foam. Your measuring cup should be ¾ full of foam. This is why it makes a difference in your recipe. If it doesn't foam, your baking powder may be old. After the foaming process has worked, pour this into the salmon mixture. Mix again with fork. It will be very thin this time. Pick up 2 iced tea spoons, dip a half-spoonful of the mixture and scoop it out with the other spoon into a deep fryer half-full of hot oil. These tidbits don't have to be turned. They will float on top of the hot oil. They turn themselves as they cook and are completely done in just a few seconds.

Recipe for Happiness

take 2 heaping cups
   of patience
1 heartful of love
2 handfuls of
   generosity

1 headful of
   understanding
dash of laughter

Sprinkle generously with kindness. Add plenty of faith and mix well. Spread over a period of a lifetime and serve everybody you meet.

International Dishes

Doukhobor Favorites

"Doukhobor Favorites" is a collection of favorite recipes used by Doukhobor women in our community.

In the Doukhobor culture recipes were never written down, but rather passed on from generation to generation. Many of the recipes were brought by our ancestors from Russia in 1893, but with new and more abundant materials in this country, they evolved into different and better recipes.

Pot of Borscht

1 cup chopped onion
1 cup butter
5 cups canned tomatoes
¼ cup water
5 cups chopped cabbage
¾ cup diced carrot
3 qt. water
3 halved potatoes, (1½ cups mashed)

2 tbsp. salt
1 small beet
1½ cups cubed potatoes
1 stalk celery, diced
1½ cups whipping cream pepper to taste
3 green onions, chopped
1 green pepper, chopped
2 tbsp. dill, chopped

Sauté onions in ¼ cup butter until clear, add canned tomatoes. Cook and stir to keep from burning. Melt ¼ cup butter with ¼ cup water in another pan, and add cabbage and carrots. Add some of the cooked tomato to this. Cook 10 minutes. Let stand. In a large soup pot, boil 3 quarts of water, add 3 halved potatoes, (to make 1½ cups mashed), 1 small beet and 1 tbsp. of salt. Remove potatoes when cooked, mash with ½ cup butter. Meantime put 1½ cups cubed potatoes into beet pot, boil 2 minutes, then add celery. To mashed potatoes, add black pepper, whipping cream and about 2 cups cooked tomatoes. Then add potato mixture and tomatoes to pot. When it comes to a boil, add cabbage and 1 tbsp. salt. Return to a boil. Remove and discard beet. Take off stove and sprinkle with green onion, green pepper and dill. Let stand about ½ hour before mixing everything. See photograph page 80.

Summer Borscht

½ lb. butter
5 cups tomatoes, canned
1 green pepper, diced
2½ cups diced onion
4 qts. water
2 tbsp. salt
4 medium potatoes, halved
½ cup grated carrots
3 cups shredded spinach
3 cups shredded beet greens
2 cups whipping cream
3½ cups diced potatoes
1 cup diced carrots
1 cup diced celery
¼ cup chopped green onion
¼ cup chopped dill

Put ⅓ of the butter into a large frying pan. Add canned tomatoes, ½ of the diced green pepper, 1 cup diced onions and simmer until thick.

In a large pot boil 4 quarts water, add 2 tbsp. salt, the tomato mixture, reserving about 1 cup of the tomato mixture, the potatoes, ½ cup diced onions. Cook until tender.

Put ⅓ of the butter into a frying pan, add ½ cup grated carrots, 1 cup diced onion and sauté. Shred spinach leaves and beet leaves finely. Place into large bowl, pour boiling water over leaves. Let stand 5 minutes and drain well. Set aside. When potatoes are tender, remove from pot and mash them. Add the ⅓ butter to the mashed potatoes, add the reserved tomatoes and half the sautéed onions and carrot mixture. Set aside.

To the boiling water in pot, add whipping cream, 3½ cups diced potatoes, the beet and spinach leaves, ½ of the diced carrots, green pepper and celery, and bring to a boil. When potatoes are tender, add mashed potatoes and rest of the onion and carrot mixture. Bring back to boil. Take off stove. Sprinkle ¼ cup chopped green onions and ¼ cup chopped dill over top. Cover pot. See photograph on cover.

The belly will not listen to advice.

Bean Soup

5 cups cooked beans
(Roman or pinto)
16 cups water
2 tbsp. salt
3 cups canned
tomatoes
1 cup chopped onions
6 cloves garlic, minced
1 cup butter

6 potatoes, quartered
1 cup cream
1 cup diced carrots
1 cup diced celery
2 cups diced potatoes
3 green onions, diced
1 tsp. black pepper

Soak 2½ cups dry beans overnight. Bring to boil, add salt. Simmer until tender. Into frying pan, put tomatoes, onions, garlic, and ½ cup butter. Simmer for 10 minutes. To beans, add quartered potatoes until the potatoes are cooked. Take out potatoes and mash with remaining ½ cup butter, cream and then add to tomato mixture. Put aside. To the bean pot add carrots, celery, simmer until just about tender then add diced potatoes. Simmer 5 minutes; add potato, tomato, onion mixture, green onions and black pepper. Bring to boil, and remove from heat. Additional cream may be added for a richer soup.

Kwas — (Cucumber Soup)

2 cucumbers, finely
grated
3 green onions, finely
diced
6 radishes, finely diced

1 tsp. salt
4 tbsp. lemon juice
4 cups water
1 tbsp. dill weed

Combine everything. Adjust salt and lemon to taste. Serve chilled. Great as a side dish with potatoes of any kind.

Fools make feasts, and wise men eat them.

Kwas (Cold Soup)

1 stalk celery, finely diced
1 onion, finely diced
8 radishes, finely diced
1 cup mashed potatoes
1 cup creamed cottage cheese
1 cup rolled oats
1-2 qts. cold water
2 tsp. salt
juice of 1 lemon
1 cup fresh cream

Combine everything, add salt and lemon juice to taste.

Halooshki (Dumpling Soup)

18 cups water
2 tbsp. salt
4 potatoes, quartered
½ cup butter
1 cup cream
1 cup diced carrots
1 cup diced celery
2 cups diced onions
3 cups diced potatoes
pepper, to taste

Bring water and salt to boil, add quartered potatoes and cook until tender. Take out, mash with ¼ cup butter and the cream. Set aside potato mixture. To water add carrots, celery, and diced potatoes. Simmer until almost tender. Sauté diced onions in remaining ¼ cup butter until glossy and add to mashed potato. Mix dumpling batter. Then add mashed potato-onion mixture and pepper to water and bring back to boil. Mix well then add dough pieces to pot and bring to boil for 5 minutes, stirring gently. Remove from stove.

Dumplings:

1 egg, beaten
½ tsp. salt
1 cup milk
2½ cups flour
¼ tsp. baking soda
1 tsp. baking powder

In mixing bowl beat egg, salt and milk. Sift dry ingredients, add to liquid ingredients and mix well. Turn dough onto floured board and knead a few times. Divide dough in half and roll to ¼" thickness. Pinch off pieces the size of a nickle. Let sit until you add diced potatoes to soup base.

Russian Vinaigrette Beet Salad

1 tbsp. sugar
5 cups diced cooked
   beets with 1 cup
   beet juice
2 cups diced apples
1 cup cooked diced
   carrots
1 cup diced onion
1 cup diced dill pickle

2 cups cooked or
   canned kidney
   beans OR 1 cup
   cooked split green
   peas
prepared horseradish
   to taste
salt to taste

Cook beets with 1 tbsp. sugar. Drain but save 1 cup juice for salad moistness. Combine everything and chill for awhile. See photograph page 80.

Vegetable Haloonki

1 cup diced onion
½ cup diced carrots
½ cup diced celery
½ cup diced green
   beans
½ cup kernel corn
1 cup peas
3 tbsp. butter
   salt and pepper to
   taste

3 eggs
1 cup buttermilk
3 cups flour
1 tsp. salt
2 heaping tsp. baking
   powder
½ tsp. baking soda
1 pint stewed tomatoes
2 tbsp. oil
6 potatoes
   melted butter

Fry all vegetables in butter until cooked. Add salt and pepper. Cool. Prepare dumpling batter. Sift in dry ingredients and mix well. In bowl beat eggs, add buttermilk and mix. Fold in cooled vegetables. Add additional flour if dough is too thin. Let stand until you prepare potatoes. Into electric frying pan pour tomatoes and oil; layer on top 6 potatoes sliced into 4 sections each. Bring to a boil. Put heaping tablespoons of the dumpling batter over all potatoes, space dumplings a little apart. Cover with lid. Simmer ½ hour without removing lid. After cooking ½ hour, test to make sure dough is not raw. Serve along with the potatoes, tomatoes and additional melted butter.

Blintzi

3 cups milk, scalded
4 eggs
2 cups flour
4 tsp. baking powder

1 tsp. baking soda
1 tbsp. sugar
1 tsp. salt

Pour scalded, cooled milk into eggs, beating well. Sift in dry ingredients and beat well. Preheat skillet to medium hot and grease. Pour ½ cup batter into pan and tilt until batter spreads to edges of pan. Bake until bottom is browned and bubbles on top are dry. Flip over for a few seconds to brown. Remove from pan, fold in half and serve with melted butter.

Cornmeal Blintzi

½ cup warm water
1 tbsp. sugar
1 tbsp. yeast
4 cups milk
½ cup cornmeal

4 large eggs, separated
1 tbsp. salt
2 tbsp. oil
3 cups flour

This is best if batter is made about 4 hours before cooking. In small bowl, mix water, sugar and yeast. Set aside. Bring 1½ cups milk to a boil, add cornmeal, stirring constantly until mixture begins to thicken. Remove from stove. In large bowl beat egg yolks, add 2½ cups milk, salt and oil, and beat well. Stir in the milk and cornmeal mixture. Fold in yeast mixture. Gradually add flour to batter, beating with eggbeaters while adding. When all the flour is mixed in, fold in stiffly beaten egg whites. Let stand until ready to bake, stirring down once after 2 hours. Bake in same manner as described for blintzi (above). If batter is not all used the same day, it may be stored in the refrigerator covered for up to one week. However, before baking add 1 tsp. baking powder folded into the batter.

Yeast Pyrahi

4 tbsp. yeast	1 cup melted
½ cup warm water	shortening
4 tbsp. sugar	1 cup warm water
8 eggs	1 tbsp. salt
1 cup melted butter	8½ cups flour

Dissolve yeast in ½ cup water with the sugar. Beat eggs, add shortening, butter and water. Beat. Add salt. Mix in dissolved yeast and flour. Knead 3 minutes. Let rise until double in bulk and punch down. Repeat rising and punching down second time. Let rise a third time, then form into balls the size of a small egg and place on floured board. Roll each ball out into a circle about 3½" in diameter. Place about 2 tbsp. filling on circle, bring the edges towards the center over the filling so they are almost touching forming an oval shape. Place on lightly greased cookie sheets about 2" apart, let rise for about 1 hour. Bake at 400°F until lightly browned, 20 to 25 minutes. Serve hot with melted butter and sour cream. They can be frozen. See photograph page 80.

Fillings for Pyrahi:

Cottage cheese: To 3 cups dry cottage cheese, add 3 eggs and salt to taste. Mix well.

Beans: Cook pre-soaked beans until soft. Mash very well, using a little cream and bean juice to make mixture softer. Add salt and sugar to taste.

Beet: Cook and peel beets, Grate finely, add butter, sugar and salt to taste. Beat slightly in frying pan.

Peas: Cook split peas or frozen green peas until soft. Mash well, add a little butter, salt and sugar to taste.

Potato: Peel and boil potatoes. Mash well and add salt to taste. Cool and add beaten eggs to make soft filling. You could add minced garlic or finely sautéed onion with a dash of black pepper.

Sauerkraut: Drain sauerkraut. Fry lightly with butter.

Pumpkin: To cooked pumpkin add brown sugar, pinch of salt, and butter. Fry until thick.

Nalesniki

1½ cups milk
½ cup whipping cream
⅓ cup warm water
1 tsp. sugar
1 tsp. yeast
4 eggs

1 tsp. salt
1¼ cups flour
1 tsp. baking powder
1½ cups half and half
    cream
¼ lb. butter, melted

Mix together the milk and cream, scald and cool. Dissolve the yeast in the water and sugar. Beat the eggs, add the cooled milk and the dissolved yeast. Add the salt and the flour, mixing well so there are no lumps. The batter will be fairly thin. Let rise only 10 minutes. Add the baking powder just before baking. Preheat a small cast iron frying pan, grease lightly. Pour about 1 tbsp. of batter into the center of the heated pan. Tilt and turn the pan rapidly to spread the batter evenly over the bottom. Set directly over the heat. Let cook about half a minute, until surface is set and bottom dry enough to come away from the pan with ease, and browned to taste. Turn the crêpe and cook on the second side about 5 seconds. Remove, spread with filling (recipe below), and roll up jelly-roll fashion. Place in well greased pan. These may be frozen at this time. When you wish to serve them, preheat oven to 400°F, mix together cream and melted butter. Pour evenly over the nalesniki, cover and bake for about 15 minutes. See photograph page 80.

Filling:

2 lbs. dry cottage
    cheese
6 eggs

salt to taste

Mix well and use about 1 tbsp. per nalesniki for filling. This recipe makes about 3½ dozen nalesniki.

A friend is one who knows your faults yet loves you in spite of your virtues.

Potato Cheese Vareniki

1 cup buttermilk
1 tbsp. oil
1 egg
2½ cups flour

¼ tsp. baking soda
½ tsp. baking powder
1 tsp. salt

Combine liquid ingredients; sift in dry ingredients and mix dough well. Turn out onto a very well floured board and roll to the thickness of a piecrust. Cut into 2½" circles. Fill dough with 1 tbsp. of filling (recipe follows) and pinch edges together to close. Drop triangles into a pot containing about 4 quarts of boiling salted water. Bring to a boil and cook for approximately 4 minutes. Remove with slotted spoon and put into the sauce (recipe follows) to keep hot. Serve together with the sauce.

Filling:

potatoes to make 2¾ cups mashed
1 medium onion, finely diced
2 tbsp. butter

1 cup grated Cheddar cheese
1 egg
salt to taste

Boil and mash potatoes to make 2¾ cups. Sauté onion in butter. Add onion, Cheddar cheese, egg, to the mashed potatoes and salt to taste. Mix well.

Sauce:

3 tbsp. butter
1 onion, finely diced
5 cups canned tomatoes

3 tbsp. cream
salt and pepper to taste

Fry onion in butter until transparent. Add canned tomatoes and simmer until thickened. Add cream, salt and pepper to taste. Bring to a boil then reduce heat and keep hot as the cooked vareniki are added to it. See photograph page 80.

Cheese Vareniki

3 eggs, lightly beaten
2 tbsp. oil in cup with
 buttermilk to make
 2 cups
1 tsp. salt
1 tsp. baking soda

1 tsp. baking powder
4 cups flour
 melted butter
2 onions, diced
½ cup butter
1 cup cream

Combine liquid ingredients, sift in dry ingredients and mix dough well. Turn out onto a very well-floured board and roll to thickness of pie crust. Cut into 2½" circles and fill dough with 1 tsp. filling. Pinch edges together to close. Drop into pot containing 4 quarts boiling, salted water. Return to a boil and cook 4 minutes. Remove to serving dish with slotted spoon and add some melted butter to keep from sticking together. Fry onions in butter until transparent. Add cream, bring to a boil and pour over vareniki. Bake at 400°F for 15 minutes.

Cottage Cheese Filling:

3 cups dry cottage
 cheese

1 tsp. salt
2 eggs

Combine all ingredients and mix well.

Fresh Fruit Vareniki

Fresh Fruit Filling:

Prepare dough as for cheese vareniki, above.
Slice fruit (strawberries, raspberries or huckleberries), put teaspoon of fruit on circle, add 2 tsp. sugar, or as much as desired, fold over and pinch edges. Cook as for cheese vareniki above, omit the butter-onion sauce. Fruit vareniki should be served with fresh cream or whipping cream.

77

Cream of Lapsha Soup

3 cups milk
1 tbsp. butter

½ tsp. salt
2 cups homemade
noodles

Bring milk to a boil on medium heat. Add butter, salt and noodles. Turn heat down and simmer for 7 minutes. Serve like soup.

Homemade Lapsha Noodles

12 large eggs
¾ cup melted butter
1 cup boiling water

1 tbsp. salt
10 cups flour

Beat eggs, add butter, water and salt and continue beating. Add flour. Knead dough for 15 minutes. Cut into pieces the size of walnuts and put through noodle machine twice to flatten very thin in long sheets. Dry the sheets on top of stove, griddle or in an oven, then put through cutters on thinnest point. See photograph page 80.

Lapshevnik (Noodle Cake)

2 cups homemade
noodles
7 eggs, separated
½ cup sweet cream

½ tsp. salt
1 tsp. baking powder

Boil noodles in salted water for 5 minutes, drain well. Pour cold water over drained noodles so they don't stick together. To beaten egg yolks, add cream, salt, baking powder and noodles, mixing well. Fold in well beaten egg whites. Pour into a greased 9" x 9" pan and bake at 400°F for 15 to 20 minutes, or until golden brown. Serve at once with melted butter

Kartoshnik (Potato Cake)

4 cups mashed
   potatoes
5 eggs, separated
1 tsp. salt

1 cup cream
3 tsp. baking powder

Mix potatoes, egg yolks, salt and cream. Beat egg whites until stiff and fold into mixture. Add baking powder and pour into a 9" x 12" greased pan. Heat oven to 400°F. Bake for 25 to 30 minutes or until golden. Serve with melted butter.

Doukhobor Cookies

¾ cup shortening
½ cup sugar
2 eggs
1 tsp. baking soda

1½ cups sour cream
3 cups flour
3 tsp. baking powder
1 tsp. salt

Cream together shortening, sugar and eggs. Add baking soda to sour cream and then add sour cream to the shortening mixture. Sift together dry ingredients and add to the batter, mixing only until no flour shows. Do not overmix. Turn dough out on lightly floured board and divide in half. Pat each half out to 1" thickness, cut out circles with cookie cutter or glass, place on cookie sheet and bake at 400°F for 10 minutes or until lightly browned. Do not overbake. Variation: Pat dough down to about 1", spread with soft butter and sprinkle brown sugar and cinnamon over top. Fold each half toward the center so that it resembles a log. Cut into 1" pieces and bake as above.

"The great secret of successful marriage is to treat all disasters as incidents and none of the incidents as disasters."

Fruit Tarts

1 cup shortening
4 cups flour
1 tsp. salt
½ tsp. baking soda
1 tsp. sugar

1 tsp. baking powder
1½ cups sour cream
½ cup buttermilk
2 eggs

Cut shortening into dry ingredients. Combine sour cream, buttermilk, and eggs. Mix into flour mixture just until blended. Roll dough out, cut to fit tart or muffin pans, and line the pans. Put in prepared Fruit Filling (below). Bake at 420°F for 15 minutes. See photograph opposite.

Fruit Filling:

1 cup Baker's starch or cornstarch
5 cups sugar

fresh fruit of your choice (see method)

Combine starch and sugar. For fruit tarts, mix 5 cups fruit and 1 cup sugar mixture, adding more plain sugar to taste. Mix all together until glossy. Fill tart shells and bake. For pie filling use 4 cups fruit and 1 cup mixture.

Plove (Rice Pudding)

3 cups rice
2 cups raisins
juice of 1 lemon
salt to taste

½ cup sugar
¾ cup melted butter
½ cup cream

Wash rice and raisins and drain. Put raisins in bowl and pour boiling water over them. Set aside. Into pot put 12 cups water, juice of 1 lemon, salt and rice, and boil until almost done. Strain rice and run hot water over it. Drain raisins. Butter casserole dish or small roaster, alternate layers of rice and raisins, sprinkling with sugar and butter until all is used up. Pour cream over and bake at 325°F for 45 minutes.

1. Fruit Tarts, Page 80
2. Homemade Lapsha Noodles, Page 80
3. Nalesniki, Page 75
4. Potato Cheese Vareniki, Page 76
5. Pot Of Borscht, Page 68
6. Russian Vinaigrette Beet Salad, Page 72
7. Vegetable Pyrahi, Page 74

Taco Salad

2 cups shredded lettuce
1 cup cooked kidney beans, drained
1 tbsp. chopped green chili pepper
½ cup sliced olives, drained
2 fresh tomatoes, chopped and drained
1 large avocado, mashed
1 cup sour cream
2 tbsp. Italian salad dressing
1 tbsp. instant minced onion
¾ tsp. chili powder
salt and pepper to taste
1 cup shredded Cheddar cheese
½ cup coarsely crushed corn chips

Combine lettuce, beans, chili, pepper, olives and tomatoes. Chill. In a separate bowl combine avocado, sour cream, salad dressing, onion and seasonings. Mix and chill. When ready to serve, top vegetables with dressing and sprinkle with cheese and corn chips.

Taco Tarts

1 lb. lean ground beef
1 onion, chopped
2 stalks celery, chopped
2 tbsp. butter
4 oz. can tomato sauce
½ tsp. garlic powder
1 tsp. chili powder
dash of cumin
salt and pepper
pastry in quantity for 2 crust pie
Cheddar cheese, grated
toppings (see below)

Brown beef with rest of ingredients, except pastry, cheese and toppings. Make your favorite pie crust recipe. Sprinkle bread board with corn meal and roll out dough. Cut circles to fit tart pans. Place dough in tart pan. Spoon 1 heaping tbsp. of filling inside and top with a small dough cut-out. Bake at 350°F for 10 minutes. Sprinkle a bit of grated Cheddar cheese over each tart. Bake another 10 minutes until cheese is melted and filling is bubbling. May be topped with chopped olives, lettuce, tomato or taco hot sauce.

Taco Shells

1½ cups cold water
1 cup flour
½ cup cornmeal

¼ tsp. salt
1 egg
vegetable oil, for
   deep frying shells

Beat all ingredients except oil with hand beater until smooth. Heat 8" skillet just until hot. Grease if necessary. To test, sprinkle with few drops water. If bubbles skitter around pan, heat is right. Pour scant ¼ cup batter into skillet. Rotate pan to spread batter very thinly. Cook until dry around edge, about 2 minutes. Turn and cook 2 minutes more. Heat 1" deep oil to 375°F. Slide tortilla into oil. Fold in half with forks and hold. Do not over fry. Shell should not be like a crisp corn chip.

Tex Mex Dip

2 cups dried beans
6 cups salted water
4 cloves garlic
1 tsp. cumin
2 or more hot jalepeño
   peppers
2 cups shredded
   cheese
1 cup sour cream
½ cup mayonnaise

1 pkg. taco seasoning
   mix
shredded cheese
3 green onions
1 green pepper, cut
   into strips
2 tomatoes, cut into 4
   sections each
12 black olives, pitted

Soak garbanzo or any dried beans in plain water overnight. Drain. Cook beans in salted water. In last ½ hour, add garlic, cumin, and peppers, according to your taste. Drain some liquid from beans and blend beans in blender. Mixture should be creamy. Refry with cheese, just until cheese melts. Chill. Place on platter. Mix sour cream, mayonnaise, and taco seasoning mix. Spoon on top of beans. Top with shredded cheese, green onion curls, green peppers, tomatoes, olives. Cut most of white part of onion off, leaving 1" white base, 2" green stem. Split stems into many tiny slivers, to curl up. Set into center of dip. Serve as a dip with taco chips. See photograph page 16.

Beef Tacos

3 tbsp. salad oil
2 lbs. ground chuck
¾ cup minced onion
½ tsp. oregano
¼ tsp. cumin
2 cloves garlic, minced
1 tsp. minced chili
   peppers
2 tsp. chili powder

2 tsp. salt
¼ tsp. pepper
2 cups beef stock
7½ oz. can tomato sauce
2 cups shredded
   lettuce
1 cup grated cheese
16 taco shells

Brown meat in oil. Add onion and sauté. Stir in seasonings and cook 5 minutes. Add stock and tomato sauce. Simmer, uncovered, ¾ hour or until sauce is thick, cook longer if necessary. Spoon beef mixture into taco shells and top with shredded lettuce and grated cheese.

Refried Beans

2 cups water
8 oz. dried pinto beans
   (1¼ cups)
1 medium onion
   chopped
¼ cup butter

¾ tsp. salt
½ cup shredded
   Cheddar cheese
chili powder,
   cayenne, garlic, if
   desired

Mix water, beans and onion. Cover, heat to boiling, boil 2 minutes. Remove, let stand 1 hour. Add enough water to beans to cover. Boil gently until beans are tender. Mash beans, stir in butter, salt, cheese and spices, if desired.

Tomato-Chili Sauce:

2 medium tomatoes,
   finely chopped
1-3 jalapeño peppers,
   finely chopped

1 medium onion, finely
   chopped
1 tsp. salt
¼ tsp. cumin powder
¼ tsp. garlic powder

Mix all ingredients. Cover, keep in refrigerator up to 1 week.

Home-Style Tacos

4 eggs
½ cup butter, melted
½ cup boiling water

½ tsp. salt
5 cups flour

Beat eggs, butter, water and salt. Gradually add enough flour to make a stiff dough. Roll out ⅛" thick. Cut into 6" circles. Deep fry in enough oil to cover. Place each circle onto paper towels into a clean paper bag to absorb excess oil. Have following toppings ready and let everyone add their own:

— grated cheese, white and yellow
— fried mushrooms
— cooked, seasoned hamburger (optional)
— shredded lettuce
— pitted olives
— diced tomatoes
— diced raw onions
— sliced avocado
— salsa sauce, or stewed thick spicy tomatoes (added last over top)

To reheat shells, put into 300°F oven for 15 minutes. They will be crisper. These tacos do not fold up, you eat them with a knife and fork. See photograph on cover.

Mexican Salsa Sauce

2 hot red chilies, seeded and cut into pieces
2 cups canned tomatoes
2 medium onions, chopped

2 cloves garlic
1 tsp. ground coriander
½ tsp. sugar
½ tsp. salt
1 tbsp. wine vinegar
1 tbsp. chopped parsley

Combine the chilies, tomatoes, onion, garlic and spices in blender until smooth. Add vinegar and parsley. Serve hot or cold with chicken, fried eggs or tacos.

Meatless Enchiladas

Tortillas:

1 cup sifted flour
½ cup corn meal
½ tsp. salt

1 egg
1½ cups cold water

Tortilla Filling:

2 cups grated sharp
   yellow cheese

1 cup minced onion
½ tsp. salt

Enchilada Sauce:

28 oz. can tomatoes
2 tbsp. oil
2 tbsp. minced onion
2 cloves garlic, minced
1 tbsp. flour
3 tsp. chili powder

1 tsp. salt
1 tsp. crushed red
   peppers
dash of cumin
2 tsp. white vinegar
¼ tsp. Tabasco

To make tortilla filling, grate cheese; mince onion. Mix cheese, onion, and salt thoroughly. Cover and set aside. Prepare enchilada sauce. Drain tomatoes, reserving ¾ cup of juice. In saucepan, brown onion and garlic in oil until golden. Stir in flour until smooth. Add tomato juice, tomatoes and seasonings. Cover and simmer until thickened. Prepare tortillas. Combine flour, corn meal, salt, egg and water in a large mixer bowl and beat with electric mixer on low speed until smooth. Pre-heat electric griddle or frying pan to 375°F. Spoon batter, 3 tbsp. at a time onto the hot, ungreased surface. Spread batter to make very thin, 6" pancakes. Turn tortillas when edges begin to look dry, not brown. Bake other side and keep warm in covered pan. Batter should yield 12 tortillas. To prepare enchiladas, place a large spoonful of tortilla filling on each tortilla; roll up. Arrange, seam down in a 13" x 9" x 2" baking dish. Cover with enchilada sauce and sprinkle with any remaining filling. Bake in 350°F oven, 25 to 30 minutes, or until hot and bubbling. Enchiladas may be prepared in advance and refrigerated or frozen. Additional baking time is required for chilled or frozen enchiladas. Allow about 1¼ hours to heat when frozen. Makes 4 to 6 servings.

Burritos (Meatless)

Flour tortillas:

2 cups flour
1 tsp. baking powder
1 tsp. salt

½ cup shortening
¾ cup water (approx.)

Sift dry ingredients together into mixing bowl. Cut in shortening. Add enough water to make a soft dough. Divide dough into 12 equal parts and roll out thinly on a floured board to 8" diameter. Bake on lightly greased frying pan, turning frequently to cook through. Makes 1 dozen 8" tortillas.

Filling:

1 qt. cooked beans
1 cup grated Cheddar
    cheese
2 tbsp. butter

4 oz. can Ortega green
    chili sauce
1 medium tomato,
    finely diced
1 small onion, finely
    diced

Heat beans and mash. Add cheese and butter. Stir until cheese is melted. Combine sauce, tomato and onion. Place 2 tbsp. of beans on each tortilla and top with chili sauce. Roll. Eat as is or fry rolled tortilla until golden brown in butter.

"You must always be prepared to do new things ... Women shouldn't think that they can't have everything. You don't have to give up a family to be successful. You can do it all. Only you won't get much sleep."

Rio Grande Pork Roast

4-5 pound boneless pork
    loin roast
½ tsp. salt
½ tsp. garlic salt
½ tsp. chili powder

½ cup apple jelly
½ cup ketchup
1 tbsp. vinegar
½ tsp. chili powder
1 cup crushed corn
    chips

Place pork, fat side up, on rack in shallow roasting pan. Combine the salt, garlic salt, and the first ½ tsp. chili powder; rub into roast. Bake in 325°F oven for 2 to 2½ hours. In small saucepan, combine jelly, ketchup, vinegar, and the remaining chili powder. Bring to boiling; reduce heat and simmer, uncovered, for 2 minutes. Brush roast with glaze; sprinkle top with corn chips. Continue roasting 10 to 15 minutes more. Remove roast from oven. Let stand 10 minutes. Measure pan drippings, including any corn chips. Add water to make 1 cup. Heat to boiling and serve with meat.

Minute Steaks Parmesan

1 egg
1 tbsp. water
    dash pepper
¼ cup finely crushed
    saltine crackers (6
    to 7 crackers)

¼ cup grated Parmesan
    cheese
5 beef cube steaks
    (about 4 oz. each)
¼ cup cooking oil
8 oz. can pizza sauce

Beat together egg, water, and pepper. Combine crumbs and half the cheese. Dip steaks in egg mixture, then in crumbs. In skillet, brown steaks in hot oil. Drain on paper toweling. Arrange steaks in 10" x 6" x 1½" baking dish; cover with pizza sauce and sprinkle with remaining cheese. Bake in 325°F oven for 20 minutes. Makes 5 servings.

Chicken Saltimbocca

3 large chicken breasts, skinned, boned, and halved
6 thin slices ham
3 slices mozzarella cheese, halved
1 medium tomato, seeded and chopped
½ tsp. dried sage, crushed
⅓ cup fine dry bread crumbs
2 tbsp. grated Parmesan cheese
2 tbsp. snipped parsley
4 tbsp. butter, melted

Place chicken, boned side up, on cutting board. Place a piece of clear plastic wrap over. Working from the center out, pound lightly with meat mallet to 5" x 5". Remove wrap. Place a ham slice and half slice cheese on each cutlet, cutting to fit. Top with some tomato and a dash of sage. Tuck in sides and roll up jelly-roll style, pressing to seal well. Combine bread crumbs, Parmesan, and parsley. Dip chicken in butter, then roll in crumbs. Place in shallow baking pan. Bake in 350°F oven 40 to 50 minutes. Serves 6. See photograph page 64.

Pizza Dough

6 cups sifted flour
4 tbsp. baking powder
1½ tsp. salt
¾ cup shortening
milk

Sift dry ingredients together. Cut in shortening. May be refrigerated in covered jar up to 14 days. For each pizza, combine 2 cups mix with ¾ cup milk, mixing lightly with a fork. Turn out on floured board and knead dough and crumbs together. Roll out to 12" circle. Bake until brown for 15 minutes, put filling on, then bake another 20 minutes.

Raised Pizza

1 cup warm water	4 tbsp. oil
2 tsp. sugar	2 tsp. salt
1 tbsp. yeast	2 cups flour

Put warm water in bowl, stir in sugar, add yeast. Let stand 10 minutes. Stir well; add oil, salt and ¾ cup flour. Beat until smooth. Stir in additional 1½ cups flour to make soft dough. Knead 8 minutes. Place in greased bowl. Cover. Let rise ½ hour. Punch down and divide dough. Roll thin. Fill with filling and bake 30 minutes at 350°F, or bake crust first then add filling.

Pizza Filling

1 cup diced onion	1 tsp. pepper
1 cup diced celery	1 tsp. salt
4 cloves garlic	1 green pepper, sliced
¼ cup oil	10 oz. can olives, sliced
1 qt. canned tomatoes	10 oz. can mushrooms, drained
6 oz. can tomato paste	¼ lb. mozzarella cheese
1 pkg. spaghetti mix OR 1 tsp. each of oregano, marjoram and basil	¼ lb. grated Cheddar cheese
	slices of thin sausage

Fry onions, celery, garlic in oil until tender; add tomatoes, paste and spices. Simmer ½ hour until thickened. Cool. Spread on pizza crust. Sprinkle with cheeses. Top with green pepper circles , mushrooms, olives, sausages, or anything you like.

"The modern wife is one who knows what her husband's favorite dishes are — and the restaurants that serve them."

Lasagne

½ lb. ground beef
½ lb. ground sausage
   meat
1 recipe Basic Tomato
   Sauce (below)

½ lb. ricotta or cottage
   cheese
¾ cup Parmesan cheese
6 oz. sliced mozzarella
   cheese
½ lb. lasagne noodles

Fry ground beef and sausage meat until lightly browned and crumbly. Drain off excess fat. Add meat to basic tomato sauce; simmer covered for 45 minutes. Meanwhile cook lasagne noodles in boiling salted water for 10 to 15 minutes. (Noodles should be slightly undercooked). Drain noodles on paper towels. To assemble lasagne, spread ¼ meat sauce in a 12" x 9" x 2" baking dish. Arrange ⅓ lasagne noodles on top. Mix cottage cheese and ½ cup Parmesan cheese. Sprinkle ⅓ cottage cheese mixture on top of noodles. Top with ¼ of mozzarella cheese. Repeat layers 2 more times finishing with meat sauce. Top meat sauce with remaining mozzarella and Parmesan cheese. Bake in a 350°F oven for 30 to 40 minutes or until lasagne is bubbly and cheese lightly browned. Allow to sit 5 to 10 minutes. Cut into squares and serve.

Basic Tomato Sauce:

2 tbsp. corn oil
¾ cup chopped onion
10 oz. can mushrooms,
   drained
3 cloves garlic,
   chopped fine
28 oz. can stewed
   tomatoes
6 oz. can tomato paste

1 bay leaf
½ tsp. basil
½ tsp. oregano
¼ tsp. marjoram
¼ tsp. rosemary,
   crushed
½ tsp. salt
⅛ tsp. pepper
1½ tsp. sugar

Sauté onions, mushrooms, and garlic in oil until soft but not browned. Add remaining ingredients and mix well. Bring to boil; reduce heat and simmer uncovered for 1½ to 2 hours or until sauce has thickened and reduced to a 3 cup quantity.

Greek Moussaka

1 large eggplant (about 2 lbs.)
¼ cup oil
1½ cups diced onion
1 lb. ground beef
3 cloves garlic, minced
dash each cinnamon, nutmeg, cloves, basil
1 tsp. oregano
1 tsp. salt
pepper to taste
10 oz. can mushrooms, drained, sliced
3 tbsp. snipped parsley
14 oz. can tomatoes
6 oz. can tomato paste
½ cup dry red wine
2 cups mashed potatoes or uncooked scalloped potatoes
¼ cup butter
¼ cup cream
1 tsp. baking powder
1 recipe Rich Cheese Sauce

Cut eggplant in ¼" slices; sauté in oil. Remove eggplant and add to oil, onions, beef, garlic, and seasonings. Add mushrooms, parsley, tomatoes, tomato paste and red wine. Simmer ½ hour. Meanwhile boil potatoes for 2 cups mashed. Season with butter, cream, salt, pepper and baking powder. Prepare Rich Cheese Sauce, below.

Set oven to 350°F. Layer in 13" x 9" x 2" baking dish ½ of eggplant, ½ of meat mixture, potatoes, rest of eggplant, then meat. Top with cheese sauce. Bake 45 minutes. Let stand 10 minutes before cutting.

Rich Cheese Sauce:

4 tbsp. butter
4 tbsp. flour
1 tsp. salt
dash nutmeg
2 cups milk (OR 1 cup cream and 1 cup milk)
1 chicken bouillon cube
1 lb. cottage cheese OR 1 lb. ricotta OR ½ cup grated Parmesan

Melt butter in saucepan, add flour, salt, and nutmeg, stirring contantly. Stir in milk and chicken broth and cook until thickened. Slowly beat ½ of mixture into beaten eggs, then beat back into pan. Cook 1 more minute. Remove and add cheese.

Spanikopets — Greek

¼ cup olive oil
½ cup finely chopped
  onions
¼ cup finely chopped
  green onions,
  including 2" of the
  tops
  lbs. fresh spinach,
2 washed, drained
  and finely chopped,
  OR 1 lb. frozen
  cup fresh dill leaves
¼ OR 2 tbsp. dried
  dillweed

¼ cup chopped parsley
½ tsp. salt
  freshly ground
  pepper
⅓ cup milk
½ lb. Feta cheese,
  crumbled
4 eggs, lightly beaten
16 sheets (½ lb.) filo
  pastry or frozen
  puff pastry
1 cup butter

Heat olive oil, add onions and green onions, cook 5 minutes, until soft and transparent but not brown. Stir in spinach, cover tightly, cook for 5 minutes, add dill, parsley, salt and pepper, stirring; cook uncovered for 10 minutes or until spinach just begins to stick. Transfer to a deep bowl and stir in milk. When cooled add cheese and eggs. Adjust seasonings.

Heat oven to 300°F. Coat bottom and sides of 12" x 7" x 2" dish with melted butter. Line with a sheet of filo, spread butter on top, lay on another sheet of filo, more butter, etc. until 8 sheets are used.

Spread spinach mixture over filo and place other filo sheets as before. Brush the top with butter and bake for 1 hour.

"Nobody grows old by merely living a number of years; people grow old only be deserting their ideals. Years wrinkle the skin, but to give up enthusiasm wrinkles the soul."

Japanese Sukiyaki

1 lb. beef tenderloin, thinly sliced
6 green onions, in 2" pieces
1 large onion, sliced
1 lb. can bean sprouts, drained
4 large celery stalks, sliced
1/2 head Chinese cabbage, in 1/2" slices
2 lb. pkg. noodles
14 oz. can bamboo shoots, drained and sliced
1/2 cup water chestnuts, sliced
3 large mushrooms, sliced
3 pieces bean curd (tofu) (optional)
few small pieces beef suet

Arrange meat and vegetables attractively on a large tray. (This can be done ahead of time and kept in the refrigerator). Place electric skillet on table and preheat. An Oriental saucepan or large skillet may be used. Place suet in pan and rub over bottom and sides with a pair of chopsticks. When fat is hot, start putting in pieces of meat and vegetables, until about half of meat and half of the vegetables are in the pan. Just as meat starts to turn color, add a part of the sauce (below), mixing it with everything, and let cook about 5 minutes. Add tofu and continue to cook until everything is done. (Vegetables are best served crunchy). Serve with side dishes of rice. Continue to cook remaining meat and vegetables. Serves 6.

Sauce:

1/2 cup soy sauce
1/2 cup water
2 tbsp. sugar
2 tbsp. sake (optional)

About 1 hour before serving combine sauce ingredients.

The most completely lost of all days is the one on which we have not laughed.

Yakatori

½ cup soy sauce
2 tbsp. lemon juice
2 tbsp. sugar
1 clove garlic
½ tsp. ginger

2 tbsp. oil
1 tbsp. sesame seeds
2 green onions, sliced
1 lb. beef sirloin, cut in
   1" cubes

Combine everything but sirloin. Thread meat on skewers. Marinate 4 hours. Broil on pan about 2-3 minutes. Turn once. See photograph on cover.

Teriyaki Roast Tenderloin

½ cup dry sherry
¼ cup soy sauce
2 tbsp. dry onion soup
   mix

1 tbsp. brown sugar
2 lbs. beef tenderloin
2 tbsp. water

Combine dry sherry, soy sauce, dry onion soup mix, and brown sugar. Place beef tenderloin in large clear plastic bag; set in deep bowl to steady roast. Pour in marinade and close bag tightly. Let stand 2 hours or overnight in refrigerator. Occasionally press bag against meat in several places to distribute marinade evenly. Remove meat from marinade. Place tenderloin on rack in shallow roasting pan. Bake in 425°F oven for 45 to 50 minutes, basting the meat occasionally with about half of the marinade. In small saucepan, heat the remaining marinade and the water until mixture bubbles. Slice meat into ¼" thick slices and arrange on heated platter. Spoon wine sauce over slices of beef to serve. If desired, garnish platter with watercress sprigs. Makes 6 to 8 servings.

The only way to have a friend is to be one.

Vegetable Tempura

1 recipe Tempura
    Batter
12 fresh green beans, in
    2" pieces
12 fresh mushrooms
12 green onions, in
    julienne strips
1 medium sweet
    potato, pared and
    cut in ½" cubes

1 small cauliflower,
    broken into buds
1 head broccoli, broken
    into buds
1 large green pepper,
    in strips
1 recipe Dipping Sauce

Prepare Tempura Batter. Dip vegetables in batter. Fry in deep hot fat, 375°F, a few at a time, until golden, 3 to 5 minutes. Drain on paper toweling. Serve vegetables with Dipping Sauce. Makes 6 servings.

Tempura Batter:

1¼ cups beer
1⅓ cups all-purpose
    flour
2 tbsp. grated
    Parmesan cheese

1 tbsp. snipped parsley
1 tsp. salt
⅛ tsp. garlic powder
1 tbsp. cooking oil
2 eggs, separated

Let beer stand at room temperature 45 minutes or until flat. In mixing bowl, combine flour, Parmesan cheese, parsley, salt and garlic powder. Stir in cooking oil, 2 beaten egg yolks, and the beer; beat until smooth. Fold in 2 stiffly-beaten egg whites.

Dipping Sauce:

½ cup unsweetened
    pineapple juice
2 tbsp. brown sugar

2 tbsp. vinegar
1 tsp. soy sauce

Mix ingredients and heat. Makes ¾ cup.

Indonesian Spareribs

3 lbs. spareribs
¾ tsp. hickory smoked
   salt
¼ tsp. black pepper
1 tbsp. coriander seed,
   crushed
1 tbsp. cumin seed,
   crushed
1 tsp. garlic powder

1 tbsp. instant minced
   onion
½ tsp. ginger
¼ cup salad oil
1 tbsp. brown sugar
¼ cup soy sauce
¼ cup lime or lemon
   juice
3 cloves garlic

Cut spareribs into serving-size pieces. Place on rack in shallow pan. Combine remaining ingredients, mixing well. Spoon or brush sauce over ribs to coat all sides. Bake in 325°F oven 1½ hours or until ribs are tender and browned, basting with sauce several times. Serves 4 to 6.

East Indian Chicken Curry

¼ cup butter
3 cloves garlic, minced
1 cup onion, diced
3 cups chicken broth
1 chicken
¼ cup butter
2-3 tsp. curry powder
1 cup chopped apple

¼ cup flour
¼ tsp. cardamon
1 tsp. ginger
½ tsp. salt
¼ tsp. pepper
2 tsp. grated lime peel
2 tbsp. lime juice
¼ cup chutney

Sauté garlic and onion in ¼ cup butter. Set aside. Brown chicken in ¼ cup butter 5 minutes each side. Add 2 cups chicken broth and simmer 20 minutes. Remove chicken and add another cup broth to make 3 cups. Add remaining ingredients plus garlic onion mixture to make curry sauce. Then add to chicken and bake 1 hour at 350°F. Serve over rice.

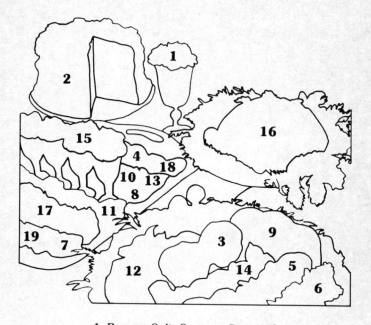

Indian Chick Peas

1 lb. chick peas
½ cup butter or
   margarine
2 onions, sliced
1½ tsp. turmeric

¼ tsp. ginger
½ tsp. chili powder
2 tomatoes, sliced
   salt to taste
   lemon juice

Wash peas and soak overnight in water to cover. Bring peas to a boil, then simmer for 1½ to 2 hours, or until tender. Drain, reserving liquid. Mash. Melt butter in a skillet. Add onion and cook over medium heat until lightly browned. Add the spices and sliced tomatoes, mixing well. Fry for 10 to 12 minutes. Add reserved liquid and the peas. Mix until blended. Taste to be sure seasonings are correct and add salt as needed. Simmer for 10 minutes longer. Sprinkle with lemon juice.

Lemon Shrimp Oriental

1 lb. frozen, shelled
   and deveined
   shrimp
5 oz. fresh mushrooms,
   sliced (2 cups)
1 medium green
   pepper, in strips
¼ cup sliced green
   onion
1½ cups bias-sliced
   celery
2 tbsp. cooking oil

6 oz. pkg. frozen pea
   pods
2 tbsp. cornstarch
1 tsp. sugar
1 tsp. salt
1 tsp. chicken bouillon
⅛ tsp. pepper
1 cup water
½ tsp. grated lemon
   peel
3 tbsp. lemon juice
   hot cooked rice

Cook shrimp, mushrooms, green pepper, onion and celery in hot oil for 5 to 6 minutes, stirring constantly. Add pea pods; cook and stir 1 to 2 minutes more. Combine cornstarch, sugar, salt, bouillon, and pepper; blend in water, lemon peel and juice. Stir into shrimp mixture. Cook and stir till thickened and bubbly. Serve over hot rice. Makes 6 servings.

Chinese Slivered Eggs

1 tbsp. vegetable oil
1 cup thinly sliced
   mushrooms
4 cups shredded
   lettuce
1 tsp. soy sauce
½ tsp. sugar
¼ tsp. salt

½ cup thinly sliced
   green onions or
   scallions
⅓ cup toasted slivered
   almonds
1 recipe Egg Pancakes,
   slivered

In the same skillet as the eggs were cooked heat the 1 tbsp. of oil over moderately high heat. Add mushrooms, lettuce, soy sauce, sugar and salt and cook, stirring constantly, about 3 minutes, until lettuce wilts. Add egg slivers and green onions, and toss gently until heated through. Sprinkle with almonds and serve. Makes 4 servings.

Egg Pancakes:

4 eggs
1 tsp. soy sauce
¼ tsp. salt

½ tsp. sugar
2 tsp. vegetable oil

In a small bowl beat eggs lightly with the soy sauce, salt and sugar. In a 10" skillet heat 1 tsp. of the oil over medium heat; when a drop of water skips across the bottom of the pan, it's ready. Pour ¼ cup of the egg mixture into the skillet, or enough to thinly coat the bottom. Cook 20 to 30 seconds, until pancake is set. Working quickly, lift edge of pancake, then grasp with fingers and turn over. Cook 20 seconds longer, until underside is lightly browned; turn onto a plate to cool. Repeat with remaining egg mixture, using remaining 1 teaspoon of oil when necessary. Stack pancakes and with very sharp knife slice into very thin slivers.

Maybe hard work won't kill a man, but on the other hand, who ever heard of anyone resting to death?

Stir-Fry Garden Vegetables

2 tbsp. oil
2 cloves garlic, minced
1 slice fresh ginger
  root, chopped OR 1
  tsp. ginger powder
1 lb. asparagus, in 1"
  diagonal slices
1/4 lb. mushrooms,
  sliced

1/2 cup sliced green
  onions
1/4 cup chicken broth or
  soy cube broth
1 tbsp. honey
1 tbsp. vinegar
1 tbsp. soy sauce
1 1/2 tsp. cornstarch

Heat oil in heavy fry pan or wok. Add garlic and ginger, then vegetables. Stir-fry until vegetables are tender-crisp. Mix remaining ingredients and add to vegetables. Stir and cook until sauce is clear. Other vegetables can be substituted to make 5 cups, e.g. broccoli, cauliflower, carrots, celery or green beans. See photograph on cover.

Oriental Broccoli

6 medium-sized fresh
  broccoli stalks
  vegetable oil
1 clove garlic, split
1/2 cup thinly sliced
  sweet red pepper

3 green onions, sliced
2-3 tbsp. soy or teriyaki
  sauce
salt
toasted sesame seeds

Thinly slice broccoli stems, discarding tougher portions of stalk. Separate florets. Pour into heavy frying pan enough oil to cover bottom. Heat thoroughly, add garlic and broccoli stems. Cover and cook quickly until partially tender, stirring occasionally. Add broccoli florets and cook until tender, but crisp. Stir in red pepper and green onions; heat through. Season with soy or teriyaki sauce and salt. Garnish with sesame seeds. Serves 6.

Almond Vegetable Chicken

oil for deep frying
1 cup almonds
¼ cup oil
2 cups onion, diced
1 can water chestnuts, diced
1 cup mushrooms, diced
2 cups broccoli, diced
½ cup peas
2 cups celery, diced
1 tsp. salt
½ tsp. pepper
1 cup chicken stock
2 cups cooked chicken, diced
1 tbsp. cornstarch
¼ cup water
2 tbsp. soy sauce

Blanch almonds in boiling water. Dry. Heat oil for deep frying. Fry almonds in hot oil until golden brown. Drain and chop. In large skillet, heat ¼ cup oil, add vegetables, salt and pepper, stirring constantly for 5 minutes. Pour in stock. Cover, cook 10 minutes. Add chicken. Blend together cornstarch, water and soy sauce. Stir 4 more minutes. Turn off heat. Sprinkle with almonds. Serves 4.

Hong Kong Chicken

1 broiler-fryer (about 3 lbs.)
¼ cup water
¼ cup dry sherry
¼ cup soy sauce
¼ cup honey
1 tbsp. ginger
6 cloves garlic
2 tsp. seasoned salt

Cut chicken into quarters; arrange in a single layer in a 13" x 9" x 2" baking dish. Mix remaining ingredients in a small bowl; pour over chicken, turning to coat on all sides; cover. Marinate chicken in refrigerator about 4 hours, or overnight. 2 hours before serving time, remove from refrigerator; let stand at room temperature 30 minutes, drain; reserve marinade. Arrange chicken, skin side up, on rack in broiler pan, or shallow baking pan. Brush generously with part of the marinade. Bake in 350°F oven, basting with remaining marinade every 20 minutes, for 1½ hours, or until chicken is tender and deep golden brown. Place on heated serving platter. Makes 4 servings.

Sweet and Sour Chicken

4 chicken breasts,
  skinned
salt and pepper
1 tsp. soy sauce
1 egg
1 cup cold water

2 chicken bouillon
  cubes OR 2 tsp.
  chicken in a mug
¼ cup apple cider
  vinegar
¾ cup flour
3 tsp. baking powder

Cut chicken into bite-sized pieces. Toss with salt, pepper and soy sauce. Marinate 2 hours. Mix egg, bouillon, pepper, water, vinegar, flour, baking powder. Beat well. Dunk chicken into batter. Fry in oil until browned. Drain on paper towels.

Sauce:

1 cup pineapple juice
14 oz. pineapple tidbits
¼ cup apple cider
  vinegar

¼ cup brown sugar
2 tbsp. cornstarch

Drain tidbits, reserving juice to mix with cornstarch. Bring other ingredients to boil; thicken with cornstarch and juice mixture. Take off stove and add pineapple tidbits.

Ginger Flank Steak

2 lbs. flank steak
¾ cup oil
¼ cup soy sauce
¼ cup honey or brown
  sugar
2 tbsp. vinegar

2 large cloves garlic,
  minced
2 tbsp. green onion,
  chopped
2 tbsp. grated ginger
  root OR 1½ tsp.
  powdered ginger

Score one side of the steak by making shallow cuts in criss-cross fashion. Combine remaining ingredients and marinate meat in sauce 24 to 48 hours. Broil or barbecue about 4 minutes on each side. Slice in thin strips across the grain. One flank steak makes 4 servings. Serve hot, or cold as appetizer.

Beef Chop Suey

1 lb. lean sirloin tip
1 tbsp. dry sherry
2 tbsp. soy sauce
2 tbsp. vegetable oil
½ cup thinly sliced carrots
½ cup thinly sliced celery
½ cup thinly sliced onion
1 cup sliced mushrooms
1 tsp. sugar
½ tsp. salt
6 tbsp. water
1 lb. can bean sprouts, drained
1 tbsp. cornstarch
1 tomato, cut in wedges
hot cooked rice

Marinate meat in sherry and 1 tbsp. of the soy sauce for 10 minutes. Broil 5 minutes on each side. Cool. Cut into very thin slices. Heat oil in a large skillet over high heat; add carrots, celery, onion and mushrooms. Cook and stir 2 minutes; add remaining soy sauce, sugar and salt. Mix well. Add ¼ cup of the water; lower heat to medium. Cover; cook 2 minutes. Add bean sprouts and sliced beef; mix well. Combine cornstarch and remaining 2 tbsp. water. Gradually stir into skillet; cook, stirring constantly, until mixture thickens and bubbles. Add tomato wedges; cook 1 minute longer. Serve at once with hot, cooked rice.

Stir-Fry Sauce

3 tbsp. brown sugar
⅓ cup cornstarch
2 tsp. ginger
4 cloves garlic
½ cup soy sauce
½ cup dry sherry
¼ tsp. red hot pepper
3 tbsp. vinegar
2½ cups beef or chicken broth

Combine everything except broth and put through blender. Pour into saucepan and bring to a boil, then add broth and return to boil. Cool. Keep refrigerated until needed. Use for any Chinese foods.

Chinese Roast Pork

3 lbs. lean pork butt
    OR pork tenderloin
6 slices fresh ginger
    root (optional)
2 stalks green onions,
    in 4" pieces
6 tbsp. dry sherry

2 cloves garlic, crushed
3 tbsp. dark soy sauce
3 tbsp. tomato ketchup
3 tbsp. chili sauce
3 tbsp. dark corn syrup
1 tsp. salt
¼ cup honey

Cut pork into strips about 5" x 1" x 1". Combine remaining ingredients, except honey, in a large flat pan. Marinate pork in sauce for at least 4 hours, turn over once halfway through. After marinating, brush with honey. Arrange in baking pan. Bake in moderate oven, 350°F, for 35 minutes. Turn heat to hot, 450°F; bake 15 to 20 minutes longer.

Garlic Spareribs

2 lbs. lean pork
    spareribs, in 2"
    lengths
1 tsp. salt
1 tsp. freshly ground
    pepper
1 medium onion,
    quartered

2 tsp. garlic salt
2 tbsp. cooking oil
1 garlic clove, chopped
1½ cup firmly packed
    dark brown sugar
1 cup honey

Place ribs in deep kettle and cover with water. Add salt, pepper and onion. Bring to boil. Simmer for 35 minutes. Remove ribs from water; place on broiler pan. Sprinkle with garlic salt. Place in oven at 475°F for 20 minutes, turning frequently. While ribs cook, prepare sauce. Place oil in heavy skillet; add chopped garlic clove. When oil is very hot, add brown sugar and honey. Stir until sugar dissolves. Simmer for about 10 minutes. Separate ribs, add to honey sauce and serve.

Cantonese Chow Mein

¾ lb. egg noodles,
  boiled 8 min.
  rinsed in cold
  water, drained
4 tbsp. oil
1 clove garlic, minced
¼ lb. shrimp, shelled,
  deveined
1 oz. bamboo shoots
4 leaves Chinese
  cabbage

2 stalks celery, bias-
  sliced
6 mushrooms, sliced
6 snow peas
1 cup stock
1 tbsp. cornstarch
1 tsp. soy sauce
1 tsp. salt
½ tsp. pepper
1 tbsp. oyster sauce
½ cup water OR stock
1 green onion, in short
  slivers

Brush 1 tbsp. oil on noodles to separate. Heat 2 tbsp. oil very hot. Put noodles in skillet, making sure noodles are separated by shaking loose with fork. Brown evenly. If noodles become hard, sprinkle a little water on them during the frying period. Remove from pan. Heat 1 tbsp. oil and put in garlic. When oil gets very hot, put in shrimp and brown. Add vegetables and mix. Pour in stock. Cover and cook 3 minutes. Blend together cornstarch, soy sauce, salt, pepper, oyster sauce and water. Add to pan. When juice thickens, turn off heat and pour mixture over noodles. Garnish with short green onion slivers. Serves 4.

Fried Rice

2 tbsp. oil
½ cup chopped onion
½ cup chopped celery
2 cups cooked pork,
  chicken, beef or
  ham, cut in strips

½ tsp. garlic salt
½ tsp. ginger
2 cups cold cooked rice
3 tbsp. soy sauce
1 cup peas
10 oz. can mushrooms,
  drained

Heat oil in skillet. Add all raw vegetables, stirring 2 to 3 minutes. Add remaining ingredients. Cook 8 minutes. You could omit meat.

Cherry Chipit Jewels

1¼ cups flour
⅔ cup packed brown sugar
¾ cup margarine
1 egg
½ tsp. salt

1½ cups mixed nuts (canned), or raisins, dates, etc.
1½ cups glazed cherries
1 cup chocolate chips

Mix flour with half of the sugar; add margarine and mix until crumbly. Press into 13" x 9" pan. Bake 15 minutes at 350°F. Beat egg, add remaining sugar and salt, and beat. Add cherries, halved or whole, whole mixed nuts and chips. Pour over baked base and press lightly. Bake 20 minutes more. Cut when cool. Crust may be doubled for thicker base.

Hawaiian Delight

Crust:

3 cups crushed graham wafers
½ cup melted butter

Combine wafers and butter. Pat into 13" x 9" x 2" pan. Bake 325°F for 10 minutes. Cool.

Filling:

3 oz. pkg. banana cream pudding
2 bananas, diced
14 oz. can crushed pineapple, drained
½ cup finely diced glazed cherries
½ cup fine coconut
1 cup whipping cream
1 cup almonds, slivered and toasted

Cook pudding according to package directions. Cool. Combine bananas, pineapple, cherries and coconut. Fold into pudding. Whip cream, fold into pudding. Pour over crust. Sprinkle with almonds. Refrigerate.

Cherry Triangles

3/4 cup sugar
5 tbsp. cornstarch
1/4 tsp. salt
2 10 oz. cans water
    packed, tart red
    cherries, drained

1 cup cherry juice
1 tbsp. butter
2 tsp. lemon juice

OR

1 can cherry, blueberry, apple or any fruit pie filling.

2/3 cup milk, scalded
1 pkg. active dry yeast
1 cup butter
2 1/2 cups sifted all-
    purpose flour

4 egg yolks, slightly
    beaten
1 tsp. salt

1/4 cup butter
1/2 tsp. vanilla

2 tbsp. cream
1 1/2 cups confectioner's
    sugar

3/4 cup chopped nuts

Mix sugar, cornstarch and salt in a saucepan. Add cherry juice and cook, stirring constantly, until thickened. Stir in butter, lemon juice and cherries. Cool.

Cool milk to lukewarm, add yeast. Cut butter into flour. Add liquid ingredients and egg yolks to dry ingredients, mix thoroughly. Turn out onto floured surface and knead about 10 times. Divide dough in half. Roll first half until large enough to cover surface of an ungreased 11½" x 17½" jelly-roll pan. Spread cooled cherry sauce over dough. Roll out second portion of dough and fit over dough and cherry sauce in pan. Pinch edges of the 2 layers of dough together gently. Allow dough to rise in warm place for about 15 minutes. Bake at 350°F for 45 to 55 minutes. Cool.

Cream together butter, vanilla and cream. Add sugar, beating until mixture is well blended. Spread frosting over partially cooled cookies. Sprinkle with chopped nuts. When cool, cut into 3" squares, then cut each square diagonally. Makes 48 cherry triangles. See photograph page 96.

Fudge Meltaways

½ cup butter
1 square unsweetened
  chocolate (½ oz.)
¼ cup granulated sugar
1 tsp. vanilla
1 egg, beaten
2 cups graham crumbs
1 cup coconut

½ cup nuts, chopped
¼ cup butter
1 tbsp. milk or cream
2 cups sifted icing
  sugar
1 tsp. vanilla
1½ squares unsweetened
  chocolate (1½ oz.)

Melt butter and chocolate in saucepan. Blend sugar, vanilla, egg, crumbs, coconut and nuts into butter-chocolate mixture. Mix well and press into ungreased pan. Refrigerate. Mix ¼ cup butter, milk, icing sugar, and 1 tsp. vanilla. Spread over crumb mixture. Chill. Melt the 1½ squares chocolate and spread evenly over chilled filling. Chill again. Cut in tiny squares before completely firm. See photograph page 96.

Crunchy Bites

2 cups rice crispies
2 cups icing sugar
1 cup peanut butter

8 tbsp. melted butter
1 cup coconut

Mix together and put into 8" x 8" pan. Make icing. Spread on squares. Chill in deep freeze and keep them refrigerated or cut up and store in freezer bag in deep freeze. See photograph page 96.

Icing:

4 squares semisweet
  chocolate (4 oz.)

2 tsp. paraffin wax
4 tbsp. butter

Melt together on low heat or in double boiler.

Mud Pie

18 chocolate sandwich
   cookies, crushed

¼ cup butter
1 qt. softened coffee
   ice cream

Mix butter and crushed cookies together. Press into dish. Chill 1 hour. Spread with ice cream and freeze. Remove and spread with filling and return to freezer. When serving, top with whipped cream, chopped nuts and a cherry. See photograph page 96.

Filling:

3 oz. unsweetened
   chocolate
¼ cup butter
⅔ cup sugar

⅔ cup milk
1 tsp. vanilla
¼ tsp. almond extract
⅛ tsp. salt

Melt chocolate with butter. Add sugar. Gradually add milk and cook over low heat for 5 minutes, add flavorings.

Grasshopper Pie

2 cups crushed
   chocolate wafers
⅓ cup melted butter
2 cups whipping cream

7 oz. marshmallow
   cream
⅓ cup or more crème de
   menthe liqueur

Crust:

Crush wafers and combine with butter. Save ¼ for topping. Pat into 8" x 12" pan. Bake 350°F for 15 minutes. Cool.

Filling:

Beat cream stiff. Fold in marshmallow cream then add crème de menthe. Spread over base. Sprinkle leftover crumbs. Freeze. See photograph page 96.

Fruit Whip Surprise

2 cups crushed graham
   wafers
½ cup butter
3 cups blueberries,
   strawberries or
   raspberries

2 tbsp. cornstarch
¾ cup sugar
4 cups miniature
   marshmallows
1 cup milk
1 cup whipping cream

Combine wafers and butter. Pat into 8" x 12" pan. Bake
350°F for 15 minutes. Cool. Cook fruit with cornstarch and
sugar. Cool. In double boiler melt marshmallows together
with milk. Cool. Whip cream until stiff. Fold marshmallows
into cream. Spread ½ of this cream mixture over crust. Put
fruit mixture on top, then the rest of the marshmallow cream
mixture. Sprinkle a few crushed wafers on top. Refrigerate.

Banana Split Squares

2 cups graham wafers
   crushed
½ cup melted butter
½ cup butter
2 cups icing sugar
1 tsp. vanilla
4 bananas, sliced and
   sprinkled with
   lemon juice

2 cups sliced
   strawberries
14 oz. can pineapple
   tidbits, drained
2 cups whipping cream
½ cup icing sugar
½ cup slivered almonds,
   toasted

Combine wafers and melted butter. Pat into 9" x 12" pan.
Bake at 350°F for 15 minutes. Cool. Beat butter, icing sugar,
egg and vanilla well and spread over cooled base. Refrigerate until set, 1 hour. Then add the following in 3 separate
layers, the bananas, then strawberries, then pineapple. Whip
whipping cream stiffly. Add icing sugar. Spread over fruit.
Top with toasted almonds. Refrigerate. See photograph page
96.

Peanut Parfait

¾ cup quick-cooking
   rolled oats
⅓ cup packed brown
   sugar
¼ cup chopped peanuts
3 tbsp. butter, melted
½ cup packed brown
   sugar

¼ cup all-purpose flour
2 cups milk
2 egg yolks, beaten
⅔ cup creamy peanut
   butter
½ tsp. vanilla

Stir together oats, the ⅓ cup brown sugar, peanuts, and butter. Spread mixture in bottom of 13" x 9" x 2' baking pan. Bake, uncovered, in 350°F oven for 15 minutes, stirring occasionally. Cool; crumble. In saucepan, combine remaining brown sugar and flour. Blend in milk and egg yolks. Cook and stir until bubbly, stir 1 minute more. Remove from heat. Stir in peanut butter and vanilla. Cover surface with waxed paper or plastic wrap to prevent skin from forming. Chill. In parfait glasses, alternate layers of pudding and oatmeal crunch mixture. Makes 5 or 6 servings. Garnish with whipped cream and a cherry. See photograph page 96.

Pink Cloud

1 cup white sugar
1½ tbsp. gelatin

1¼ cup milk

Melt all together until gelatin and sugar are dissolved. Chill ½ hour. Whip 2 cups whipping cream, 1 tsp. vanilla, 2 tbsp. sugar and above mixture. Add 1⅓ cups flaked coconut. Place in greased jelly mold. Chill 6 hours. Top with Crimson Sauce. See photograph page 96.

Crimson Sauce:

10 oz. raspberries
3 tbsp. sugar

½ cup red currant jelly
1 tbsp. cornstarch

Thaw and crush berries. Combine all ingredients. Cook to thicken. Boil 1 minute. Strain through sieve. Cool and gently pour over mold.

Dreamy Chocolate Cake

Bake your favorite chocolate cake recipe in a jelly-roll pan lined with greased foil. Bring foil up on all 4 sides to make 2" or 3" walls, for cake. Bake and cool cake.

Filling:

2 cups brown sugar
6 tbsp. flour
2 cups milk
4 beaten egg yolks

4 tbsp. butter
2 tsp. vanilla
1 cup chopped walnuts

Cook sugar, flour and milk. Stir until it comes to a boil. Cook 1 minute longer. Put some of hot mixture into egg yolks, stir, then add yolks to hot mixture, bring to a boil. Take off stove and add butter, vanilla and walnuts. Cool & spread over cake.

Frosting:

2 egg whites
1½ cups white sugar
¼ tsp. cream of tartar
1 tbsp. corn syrup

⅓ cup water
16 marshmallows
3 squares semisweet
   chocolate

Put egg whites, sugar, cream of tartar, corn syrup and water into double boiler. Cook and beat right away, scraping sides often about 10 minutes. Add marshmallows, cut up, one at a time, while still beating until melted. Spread over other filling mixture. Melt 3 squares semisweet chocolate and swirl on top of frosting. See photograph page 96.

HINTS FOR PERFECT COOKIES: Use Cookie sheet 2-3 inches narrower than the oven. Always bake in center of oven.

112

Royal Fluff Cake

Bottom layer Orange cake:

2 cups flour
1 cup sugar
1 tsp. salt
1 tsp. baking powder

½ tsp. baking soda
½ cup shortening
1 cup orange juice
2 eggs

Combine all ingredients in large bowl. Blend at low speed until moistened. Beat 3 minutes at medium speed, scraping bowl. Pour batter into greased 11" x 15" pan. Bake 25 to 30 minutes in 325°F oven. Let cool. Prepare filling and add layers as directed below. Sprinkle with topping (below). See photograph page 96.

Filling:

8 oz. cream cheese, softened
½ cup milk
6 oz. pkg. instant vanilla pudding

14 oz. can crushed pineapple, drained
1½ cups whipping cream
½ cup icing sugar

Blend cream cheese with ½ cup milk. Reserve 1 tsp. dry pudding powder. Prepare pudding made with ½ cup less milk than directions call for. Add pudding mixture to cheese mixture. Spread on cake. Spread pineapple over cheese mixture. Beat cream until stiff with 1 tsp. pudding powder and icing sugar. Spread over pineapple.

Topping:

1½ tbsp. butter
3 tbsp. brown sugar

pinch salt
¾ cup flaked almonds

Heat butter and sugar until melted. Add salt and almonds. Simmer until lightly brown. Cool. Crunch or break up over cake.

Black Forest Cherry Torte

2 egg whites
½ cup granulated sugar
1¾ cups sifted cake flour
1 cup granulated sugar
¾ tsp. baking soda
1 tsp. salt
⅓ cup cooking oil
1 cup milk
2 egg yolks
2 squares (2 oz.) unsweetened chocolate, melted and cooled

Cherry Filling OR 4 cups Cherry Pie Filling
Chocolate Buttercream
1 tsp. unflavored gelatin
2 tbsp. cold water
3 cups whipping cream
½ cup kirsch or cherry liqueur
1 square semisweet chocolate, shaved
¾ cup toasted sliced almonds

Cake: Beat egg whites until soft peaks form. Gradually add the ½ cup sugar, beating to stiff peaks. Into large mixer bowl sift together cake flour, 1 cup sugar, soda, and salt. Add oil, and ½ cup of the milk, beat 1 minute at medium speed. Add remaining milk and egg yolks; beat 1 minute. Fold in egg whites. Pour a third of the batter into greased and floured 9" round cake pan. Fold 2" squares cooled melted chocolate into remaining mixture in bowl. Pour chocolate batter into 2 greased and floured 9" round cake pans. Bake all layers in 350°F oven for 20 to 25 minutes. Cool in pan 10 minutes. Remove and cool on wire rack.

To make Cherry Filling:

2 16 oz. cans pitted tart red cherries, reserving ⅔ cup juice
⅔ cup granulated sugar
¼ cup cornstarch
1 tsp. vanilla

Drain cherries, (reserve juice). Combine sugar and cornstarch. Stir in reserved juice. Cook and stir until thickened and bubbly. Add cherries; cook 2 minutes. Remove from heat; stir in vanilla. Cool.

Continued on next page.

Black Forest Cherry Torte

To make Chocolate Buttercream:

3 tbsp. butter
1 cup sifted powdered
  sugar
1 square unsweetened
  chocolate, melted

2 tbsp. cream
1 tsp. vanilla
1 cup sifted powdered
  sugar

Cream butter and sugar. Beat chocolate and cool. Gradually beat in another cup sugar. Add enough cream to make a piping consistency.

To assemble cake: Soften gelatin in water; dissolve over low heat. Set aside but do not cool. In large mixer bowl whip cream until slightly thickened. Add gelatin all at once; continue beating until soft peaks form. Place one chocolate cake layer on serving plate. Fit pastry bag with medium rose point; fill with chocolate buttercream. Starting a third of the way out from center of cake, pipe a 3-inch-diameter ring of buttercream. Pipe a second ring two-thirds of the way from center. Pipe a third ring around outer edge of cake. Fill in area between buttercream with ⅓ of the cherry filling. Spread a thin layer (about 1 cup) of whipped cream over top. Place yellow cake layer atop; drizzle with Kirsch. Put about 1½ cups of the whipped cream in pastry bag with large rosette tip; pipe a band of whipped cream 2 inches wide around outer edge of cake layer. Fill center with another ⅓ of cherry filling; top with second chocolate layer. Frost cake with remaining whipped cream. Spoon remaining cherry filling in 6" circle over cream; sprinkle shaved chocolate around edges. Press toasted sliced almonds onto side of cake. Chill cake 2 to 3 hours. Makes 16 servings. See photograph page 96.

"Anything that is greatly admired is bound to be much maligned as well. Chocolate is no exception."

Holiday Fruit Cake

2¼ cups whole-wheat
    flour
1 tsp. cinnamon
½ tsp. allspice
½ tsp. nutmeg
¼ tsp. cloves
⅛ tsp. ginger
½ tsp. salt
½ cup honeyed lemon
    or orange peel
1 cup dates
1 cup dried pineapple
1 cup dried apricots
1½ cups dark raisins

1 cup light raisins
1½ cups walnuts
1 cup butter
½ cup honey
¼ cup molasses
6 eggs, separated
1 tbsp. vanilla
½ cup apple juice, plus
    extra for storing
    fruit cakes
whole blanched
    almonds for
    decoration

Prepare 2-9" x 5" loaf tins by lining them with buttered brown paper. Let the paper extend above the long sides of the pan about 2". Combine 1¾ cups whole-wheat flour with the spices and salt. Set aside ½ cup of flour mixture. Cut all fruit except raisins into small pieces. Sprinkle and separate cut fruit with reserved ½ cup flour. Chop walnuts coarsely and add to fruit. Preheat oven to 275°F. Cream butter until soft. Beat in honey and molasses. Add egg yolks and vanilla and beat until fluffy. Add flour mixture and apple juice alternately to the butter mixture beating after each addition. Carefully fold in floured fruits and nuts. Beat egg whites until stiff but not dry and fold them carefully into the batter. Turn into prepared pans. Lay whole blanched almonds on top of each loaf in desired design. Bake in preheated oven for about 2½ hours. Cool in pan for 30 minutes. Remove from pan. Remove paper and cool completely on cake rack. Wrap in several thicknesses of cheesecloth which has been drenched with apple juice. Then wrap in waxed paper and aluminum foil and store in cool dry place. See photograph page 96.

Fabulous Fruit Cake

2½ cups flour
1 tsp. baking soda
2 eggs beaten
28 oz. mincemeat
12 oz. can sweetened
    condensed milk

2 cups mixed candied
    fruit
1 cup chopped nuts
    chopped glazed
    cherries

Preheat oven to 300°F. Grease 9" tube pan. Line with waxed paper, grease again or use 10" greased and floured bundt pan. Sift flour and baking soda. Set aside. In bowl combine remaining ingredients. Add dry ingredients. Blend well. Pour into pan. Bake 1 hour and 50 minutes. Cool 15 minutes. Turn out of pan. May be garnished with cherries and thin icing. See photograph page 96.

O'Henry Balls

1 cup peanut butter
5 tbsp. butter
1½ cups icing sugar
1 cup nuts, chopped
1 cup dates

6 oz. semisweet
    chocolate
1 tbsp. shortening
    paraffin
1 cup maraschino
    cherries, halved

Mix first 3 ingredients, add nuts and dates. Melt chocolate, shortening and a bit of paraffin. Roll peanut mixture around ½ cherry forming a ball. Dip in chocolate. Cool on waxed paper. Freeze if storing. See photograph page 96.

Chipit Haysticks

6 oz. chocolate chips
6 oz. butterscotch
    chips

1 can chow mein
    noodles
1 cup peanuts

Melt chips. Stir in noodles and peanuts. Shape with spoon on wax paper. Chill. See photograph page 96.

Chocolate Snowballs

3 oz. pkg. cream
    cheese, softened
2 tbsp. milk
2 cups icing sugar
3 cups miniature
    colored
    marshmallows

2 1 oz. sq.
    unsweetened
    chocolate
½ tsp. vanilla
    pinch salt
    flaked coconut

Combine softened cream cheese and milk. Gradually add sugar. Beat in melted chocolate, vanilla and salt. Fold in marshmallows. Drop a rounded tsp. of mixture in coconut. Shape into ball. Place on baking sheet — Chill. Makes 4 dozen. See photograph page 96.

Walnut Frosties

2 cups flour
½ tsp. soda
¼ tsp. salt
1 cup firmly packed
    brown sugar

½ cup butter
1 egg
1 tsp. vanilla

Combine flour, soda and salt. Gradually add sugar to butter in mixing bowl, creaming until light and fluffy. Add egg and vanilla. Beat well. Gradually add dry ingredients, mix well after each addition. Shape into 1" balls. Place 2" apart on ungreased cookie sheet. Make a depression in center of each cookie, place teaspoonful of topping in depression. Bake at 350°F for 12 to 15 minutes until delicately brown. See photograph page 96.

Topping:

½ cup walnuts, or other
    nuts, chopped
½ cup firmly packed
    brown sugar

¼ cup dairy sour cream

Combine everything.

Shortbread Nut Sticks

1 cup butter	½ tsp. cinnamon
⅓ cup sugar	¼ tsp. salt
¼ lb. nuts, finely chopped	6 oz. chocolate chips
1⅔ cups flour	1 tbsp. crisco

Cream butter and sugar. Chop nuts fine and add. Sift in flour, cinnamon and salt. Form dough into tiny fingers. Place on ungreased cookie sheet 1" apart. Refrigerate 2 hours. Bake at 325°F 12 to 15 minutes. Cool. Melt chocolate and crisco and dip cookie front into it. See photograph page 96.

Peanut Chip Thumbprints

1 cup shortening	1 tsp. water
1 cup brown sugar	1½ cups salted peanuts, chopped
1 egg separated	
2 cups sifted flour	½ cup cream style peanut butter
1 tsp. baking powder	1 pkg. chocolate chips

Cream shortening and brown sugar, until fluffy, mix in egg yolk, blend in sifted flour and baking powder together, gradually add to sugar mixture, blending after each addition. Combine egg white and water. Shape into balls, dip in egg white mixture, roll in chopped peanuts. Place 1" apart on cookie sheet. Make thumbprint in center of each. Add ¼ tsp. peanut butter and top with chocolate chips. Bake at 350°F for 12 to 15 minutes.

The expressions of love from your child when you give him a freshly baked cookie are treasures each mother locks in her heart.

Carrot Muffins

¾ cup oil
4 eggs
2 cups sugar
1 tsp. vanilla
3 cups flour
2 tsp. baking powder
1½ tsp. baking soda
1 tsp. salt

2 tsp. cinnamon
2 cups finely grated
    carrots
14 oz. can crushed
    pineapple,
    undrained
¾ cup walnuts, chopped

Beat oil, eggs, sugar and vanilla for 3 minutes. Sift in dry ingredients, add carrots, pineapple and walnuts. Spoon into greased muffin tins or 9" x 13" x 2" pan. Bake muffins at 325°F 15 to 20 minutes, cake pan 30 to 35 minutes. Remove from tins and ice with Cream Cheese Icing. See photograph page 96.

Cream Cheese Icing

4 oz. cream cheese,
    softened
¼ cup butter

2 tsp. lemon juice
2 cups icing sugar
1 egg white

Beat everything 7 minutes and spread on muffins or squares.

Angel Spring Glory Filling

4 egg yolks
1 tbsp. lemon rind
3 tbsp. lemon juice
½ cup sugar

⅔ cup crushed
    pineapple,
    undrained
1 pkg. Dream Whip
1 cup angel flake
    coconut

Combine yolks, rind, juice, sugar and pineapple in double boiler. Cook until it begins to thicken 15 to 20 minutes. Cool. Prepare Dream Whip and fold it and coconut into pineapple mixture. Ice angel food cake with this filling.

Waldorf Astoria Frosting

1 cup milk
5 tbsp. flour
1 cup butter (or ½ cup
    butter and ½ cup
    shortening)

1 cup icing sugar
1 tsp. vanilla

Mix flour with part of milk, then add to remainder of milk to make a smooth paste. Cook until thick, stirring constantly. Chill. Beat together butter, icing sugar, and vanilla. Add butter mixture to cold flour mixture a little at a time, beating until stiff, like whipped cream.

Supreme Frosting

6 oz. chocolate chips
⅔ cup brown sugar
3 oz. cream cheese,
    softened
½ tsp. vanilla

⅛ tsp. salt
1 egg yolk
1 cup cream, whipped

Melt chocolate chips in top of double boiler. Add sugar and rest of ingredients except cream. Beat well until creamy. Fold cream into chocolate mixture and ice cake.

"This is the twelfth time you've been to the refreshment buffet."
"Oh, that's all right. I tell everybody I'm getting something for you."

Marshmallow Frosting

2 egg whites
1½ cups sugar
¼ tsp. cream of tartar
1 tbsp. corn syrup

⅓ cup water
15 marshmallows
½ sq. unsweetened
    chocolate

Put whites, sugar, cream of tartar, syrup and water in double boiler. Cook and beat right away, scaping sides often, about 10 minutes. Add marshmallows cut up one at a time, while still beating. Spread over other mixture. Melt chocolate and swirl on top of frosting.

Sweetened Condensed Milk

½ cup ice water
½ cup instant milk

⅓ cup sugar
2 tbsp. lemon juice

Freeze beaters and bowl. Combine milk and water. Beat until stiff. Add sugar and lemon juice. Has to be used right away.

Sweetened Condensed Milk

¾ cup sugar
⅓ cup cold water

⅓ cup butter
1 cup powdered milk

Boil sugar, water and butter. Remove from heat and stir in milk to blend. This can be frozen.

"The way to take criticism is with your mind, not your emotions."

Cordially Yours

Snow Punch

6 ripe bananas
1 cup lemon juice
2 cups light cream
1 cup sugar
1 pint lemon sherbet

6 7-oz. bottles (6 cups)
   lemon-lime
   carbonated
   beverage
1/3 cup flaked coconut

Peel bananas; slice into blender container. Add lemon juice. Cover and blend until bananas are puréed (about 3 cups). Combine with cream and sugar; chill. Just before serving, add carbonated beverage, stirring gently to blend. Serve in stemmed glasses or punch cups. Top with spoonfuls of sherbet; sprinkle with coconut. Makes about 13 cups.

Holly Punch

6 oz. can frozen
   concentrated
   lemonade
6 oz. can frozen
   concentrated
   orange juice

3 cups cranberry juice
   cocktail, chilled
3 cups cold water
2/3 cup grenadine syrup
1 qt. ginger ale, chilled

Combine all ingredients except ginger ale and pour over block of ice in punch bowl. Add ginger ale. Ladle into small punch cups to serve. Makes about 24 servings. To make decorative ice block, pour water or juice into jelly mold and freeze.

Orange Julius

2 oz. vanilla instant
   pudding mix
1 egg white

1 tbsp. lemon juice
3 cups fresh orange
   juice

Whirl everything in blender. Serve with ice. See photograph page 112.

Holiday Punch

1 pt. halved
    strawberries
2 medium sliced
    oranges
1 medium lemon
1 medium lime
48 oz. can apricot nectar

48 can oz. unsweetened
    pineapple juice
3 -6 oz. cans frozen
    lemonade
    concentrate
26 oz. liquor
50 oz. ginger ale
    ice mold

In large bowl combine fruits. Add liquids. Float ice ring in bowl. 50 servings.

Sangria

2 oranges
2 lemons
2 limes
2 cups sugar
4 cups water
½ cup brandy

2 bottles dry white
    wine
4 oz. Cointreau or
    Triple Sec
10 oz. club soda
    lemon and lime slices

For syrup base chop unpeeled oranges, limes and lemons coarsely. In heavy saucepan combine chopped fruit, sugar and water. Heat and stir until sugar is dissolved, then simmer uncovered 1 hour or until reduced to about half volume. Cool, strain and add brandy and refrigerate. To serve sangria, have all ingredients chilled. In large pitcher or glass bowl, combine 1 cup syrup base with wine and liqueur. Add soda and ice just before serving. Add thinly sliced lemon and orange to each glass.

"Love doesn't just sit there, like a stone; it has to be made, like bread: remade all the time, made new."

Slush

12½ oz. frozen orange
   juice concentrate
12½ oz. frozen grapefruit
   concentrate
12½ oz. frozen lemonade
   concentrate
 2 cups water

12½ oz. frozen limeade
   concentrate
48 oz. can pineapple
   juice
40 oz. bottle vodka or
   rum
 3 mashed bananas
16 oz. can crushed
   pineapple

Mix well and freeze. When serving, add ½ glass slush. Fill glass with 7-Up and ice. It should be slushy.

Caesar Mix

48 oz. tomato juice
½ cup beef broth
 6 tbsp. lime juice
½ cup white sugar
 1 tsp. Worcestershire

2 tsp. Kosher salt
1 tsp. pepper
1 tsp. celery salt
1 tsp. dillweed
1 tsp. Tabasco
1 tsp. creamed
  horseradish

Stir all ingredients together. To serve, rub glass edge with lemon then dip into salt. Add 1 oz. vodka and fill up with juice. Serve with celery stick, ice. See photograph page 112

Frozen Daiquiri

6 oz. frozen limeade
  concentrate
6 oz. water

18 oz. rum
40 oz. lemon-lime soft
  drink

Combine everything and freeze. This has the consistency of a snow cone. Makes 2 quarts.

Pina Colada

2 oz. rum
4 oz. cream of coconut
6 oz. pineapple juice

1 oz. cream
½ cup crushed ice

Combine ingredients in blender. Pour into tall glasses and garnish with fresh pineapple or grated toasted coconut. Makes 2 drinks. See photograph page 112.

Bossa Nova Special

1 oz. Galliano liqueur
1 oz. light rum
¼ oz. apricot brandy

2 oz. pineapple juice
½ oz. white of egg
¼ oz. lemon juice

Shake well, pour into tall glass with ice cubes and decorate with fruit. See photograph page 112.

Singapore Sling

1½ oz. gin
¾ oz. cherry brandy
1 oz. lemon juice

½ oz. Grenadine
club soda

Shake first 4 ingredients with ice. Strain into tall glass. Fill with soda. Garnish with fresh fruit. See photograph page 112.

Coconut Cooler

2 oz. vodka
2 oz. orange juice
2 oz. coconut cream

7 oz. club soda
orange wheel

Blend at high speed. Pour into tall glass with ice. Garnish with orange wheel.

Banana Strawberry Dream

1 cup strawberries
6 bananas
1 cup canned coconut
   cream

1 tsp. lemon juice
4 oz. pineapple juice
   club soda
   pineapple spears

Purée in blender everything except club soda and pineapple spears. Chill. Serve in tall glass with fruit purée and club soda mixed in equal parts. Garnish with pineapple spears.

Mai Tai

1½ oz. light rum
½ oz. Triple Sec
½ oz. lime juice
½ oz. Grenadine

½ tsp. icing sugar
½ oz. almond-flavoured
   syrup (orgeat)

Blend everything in blender with cracked ice. Pour into large glass. Garnish with cherry, orange slice or wedge of fresh pineapple. Serve with a straw.

Orange Eggnog

4 eggs, separated
½ cup sugar
1 cup bourbon
   (optional)
¼ cup orange liqueur
   (optional)

½ tsp. finely grated
   orange peel
1 cup freshly squeezed
   orange juice
1 cup heavy cream
½ cup light cream
   freshly grated nutmeg

Beat egg yolks and sugar until thick. Beat in bourbon and liqueur. Stir in orange peel and orange juice, then stir in heavy cream and light cream. Beat egg whites until stiff but not dry; fold into the orange juice mixture. Pour into a chilled punch bowl and sprinkle nutmeg over top.

Tropical Chocolate

1 qt. milk
6 tbsp. cocoa
1 banana

$1/2$ tsp. vanilla
sugar to taste

Whirl in blender and heat. Serve hot with a dab of whipped cream.

Coco Aloha

Heat together:

$1\frac{1}{3}$ cups shredded coconut
2 cups milk

2 tbsp. sugar
2 cups hot strong coffee

Heat together coconut, milk and sugar. Add coffee. To serve, strain into mugs and top with cream and toasted coconut. See photograph page 112.

Blueberry Tea or Coffee

$3/4$ oz. Grand Marnier
$3/4$ oz. Amaretto
lemon juice
sugar

coffee or tea
whipped cream
maraschino cherry

Dip your cup or glass rim into lemon juice, then into sugar. Pour liqueurs into cup. Fill with coffee or tea. Stir. Top with whipped cream and cherry.

What's drinking? A mere pause from thinking!

Cafe Brulot

1 cup brandy
peel of 1 medium
orange
6 whole cloves
4 whole allspice

2 cinnamon sticks
3 tbsp. sugar
3 cups hot double-
strength coffee

On serving table, in blazer of chafing dish over direct heat, heat all ingredients except coffee until brandy is hot; carefully ignite brandy with match. Let flame for 1 to 2 minutes. Slowly pour coffee into flaming brandy. Ladle into 8 café brûlot or demitasse cups. Makes 8 servings. See photograph page 112.

Coffee Mocha

3 tbsp. sugar
1/4 cup powdered instant
coffee
1 1/2 cups water

1 sq. unsweetened
chocolate (1 oz.)
pinch of salt
3 cups milk
whipped cream

Combine first 5 ingredients in saucepan. Stir over medium heat until chocolate melts; simmer 4 to 5 minutes, stirring constantly. Add milk gradually, stir until hot. Remove from heat, beat until frothy. Serve hot in cups, spoon whipped cream on each. 3 to 4 servings. See photograph page 112.

Hot Rum

2 tbsp. brown sugar
1 tsp. allspice
1 tsp. cloves
1/4 tsp. salt
dash nutmeg

3" cinnamon sticks
2 qt. apple or
pineapple juice
1 cup rum

Simmer everything except rum for 20 minutes. Stir in rum. Strain spices. Serve in mugs with butter.

Hot Spiced Cider

3 3" cinnamon sticks
2 tsp. whole cloves
1 whole nutmeg OR ½ tsp. ground nutmeg
½ gallon (8 cups) apple cider
1 cup sugar
2 cups orange juice
½ cup lemon juice
½ cup apple brandy (optional)

Tie cinnamon, cloves and nutmeg in a small piece of cheesecloth. Combine with cider and sugar in a large saucepan. Simmer 15 minutes; remove spice bag. Stir in orange and lemon juices. Heat just until bubbly-hot. Pour into heated punch bowl. Small oranges studded with whole cloves may be added for garnish.

Burnt Almond

¾ oz. Kahlua
¾ oz. Amaretto
2 oz. cream or milk

Beat in blender. Serve with ice in tall glass.

B-52

½ oz. Kahlua
1 oz. Bavarian Cream
¾ oz. Grand Marnier

Pour into glass in order given. Pour slowly so as not to mix layers. Do not stir. Other liqueurs in different colors may be added, sip in layers. See photograph page 112.

The best way to keep your friends is not to give them away.

Tia Maria

3 cups brown sugar
2 cups water
1 tsp. vanilla

⅓ cup camp coffee
½ cup dark rum
26 oz. vodka

Boil the sugar and water gently for 10 minutes. Remove from stove and add remaining ingredients. Mix well and bottle. (Camp coffee can be purchased in a wine supplies shop.)

Amaretto Liqueur

2 cups sugar
2 cups water
2 cups vodka

2 cups brandy
4 tsp. almond extract

Simmer sugar and water 3 minutes. Cool. Add liquors and extract. Blend. Age for 2 weeks.

Exotic Liqueur

1 cup whipping cream
1 cup Scotch
1 cup sweetened
   condensed milk

½ tsp. coconut extract
1½ tbsp. Nestlés Quick
   chocolate syrup
3 eggs, well beaten

Blend 10 seconds. May be refrigerated up to 3 weeks.

One drink is plenty;
Two drinks too many,
And three not half enough.

Cocoa Vanilla Cordial

1 lb. brown sugar
2½ cups water
1 vanilla bean OR 4
    tsp. vanilla

¾ cup cocoa
1½ tsp. peppermint
    extract
1 qt. vodka

Combine first 3 ingredients and boil 10 minutes. Add cocoa, extract and vodka. Age for 2 weeks. Will keep a long time.

Bailey's Irish Cream

1 cup rye whisky
3 tsp. instant coffee
1 tsp. vanilla
1 egg
1 cup whipping cream

12 oz. can sweetened
    condensed milk
1 cup milk
pinch of cinnamon

Blend in blender. Store in refrigerator.

Vanilla Orange Liqueur

1 cup water
1 cup corn syrup
2 tbsp. dark syrup
⅓ cup sugar
peel from 2 oranges

1 vanilla bean OR 2
    tsp. vanilla
¼ cup pure orange
    extract
2 cups vodka

Combine everything except last 2 ingredients. Boil 10 minutes. Remove and stir in extract. Cool. Add vodka. Put into sealed containers. Age for 2 weeks.

Metric Equivalent Chart

Length

1 INCH (in) = 2.5 CENTIMETERS (cm)
1 FOOT (ft.) = 30 CENTIMETERS (cm)
1 MILLIMETER (mm) = .04 INCH (in.)
1 CENTIMETER (cm) = .4 INCH (in.)

Mass Weight

1 OUNCE (oz.) = 28 GRAMS (g)
1 POUND (lb.) = 450 GRAMS (g)
1 GRAM (g) = .035 OUNCES (oz.)
1 KILOGRAM (kg) or
1000 GRAMS (g) = 2.2 POUNDS (lb.)

Liquid Volume

1 FLUID OUNCE (fl. oz.) = 30 MILLILITERS (mL)
1 FLUID CUP (c) = 240 MILLILITERS (mL)
1 PINT (pt.) = 470 MILLILITERS (mL)
1 QUART (qt.) = 950 MILLILITERS (mL)
1 GALLON (gal) = 3.8 LITERS (L)
1 MILLILITER (mL) = .03 FLUID OUNCES (fl. oz.)
1 LITER (L) OR
1000 MILLILITERS = 2.1 FLUID PINTS OR
                    1.06 FLUID QUARTS OR
                    .26 GALLONS (gal.)

Index

Appetizers

Breakfasts and Brunches

Soups

Salads

Vegetables

Main Courses

International Dishes

Chinese

Italian

Basic Tomato Sauce ———————————————— 90
Chicken Saltimbocca ———————————————— 88
Lasagne ————————————————————————— 90
Minute Steaks Parmesan ——————————————— 87
Pizza Dough ———————————————————— 88
Pizza Filling ————————————————————— 89
Raised Pizza ————————————————————— 89

Japanese

Japanese Sukiyaki ————————————————— 93
Teriyaki Roast Tenderloin ——————————————— 94
Vegetable Tempura ————————————————— 95
Yakatori ———————————————————————— 94

Mexican

Beef Tacos ——————————————————————— 83
Burritos (Meatless) ————————————————— 86
Home-Style Tacos ————————————————— 84
Meatless Enchiladas ——————————————————— 85
Mexican Salsa Sauce ———————————————— 84
Refried Beans ————————————————————— 83
Rio Grande Pork Roast ——————————————— 87
Taco Salad ——————————————————————— 81
Taco Shells ——————————————————————— 82
Taco Tarts ——————————————————————— 81
Tex Mex Dip ————————————————————— 82
Tomato-Chili Sauce ————————————————— 83
Tortillas ————————————————————————— 86

Desserts

Angel Spring Glory Filling ——————————————— 120
Banana Split Squares ————————————————— 110
Black Forest Cherry Torte ——————————————— 114
Carrot Muffins ————————————————————— 120
Cherry Chipit Jewels ————————————————— 106
Cherry Triangles ————————————————————— 107
Chipit Haysticks ————————————————————— 117
Chocolate Snowballs ————————————————— 118
Cream Cheese Icing ————————————————— 120
Crimson Sauce ————————————————————— 111
Crunchy Bites ————————————————————— 108
Dreamy Chocolate Cake ——————————————— 112
Fabulous Fruit Cake ————————————————— 117
Fruit Whip Surprise ————————————————— 110

Cordially Yours

For Friends Who Love to Cook, Give

Doorway to Creative Cuisine

Please send _____ copies of
DOORWAY TO CREATIVE CUISINE at $9.95 each, plus $1.50 each for
postage and handling to:

Name: _____

Street: _____

City: _____

Province/State: _____ Postage Code/Zip
U.S. orders payable in U.S. funds

Make cheque or money order payable to:
Doorway to Creative Cuisine Publishing
R.R. #1, Site 25
Compartment 1
Castlegar, B.C.
Canada V1N 3H7

For Friends Who Love to Cook, Give

Doorway to Creative Cuisine

Please send _____ copies of
DOORWAY TO CREATIVE CUISINE at $9.95 each, plus $1.50 each for
postage and handling to:

Name: _____

Street: _____

City: _____

Province/State: _____ Postage Code/Zip
U.S. orders payable in U.S. funds

Make cheque or money order payable to:
Doorway to Creative Cuisine Publishing
R.R. #1, Site 25
Compartment 1
Castlegar, B.C.
Canada V1N 3H7

For Friends Who Love to Cook, Give

Doorway to Creative Cuisine

Please send _____ copies of
DOORWAY TO CREATIVE CUISINE at $9.95 each, plus $1.50 each for
postage and handling to:

Name: _____

Street: _____

City: _____

Province/State: _____ Postage Code/Zip
U.S. orders payable in U.S. funds

Make cheque or money order payable to:
Doorway to Creative Cuisine Publishing
R.R. #1, Site 25
Compartment 1
Castlegar, B.C.
Canada V1N 3H7

For Friends Who Love to Cook, Give

Doorway to Creative Cuisine

Please send _____ copies of
DOORWAY TO CREATIVE CUISINE at $9.95 each, plus $1.50 each for
postage and handling to:

Name: _____

Street: _____

City: _____

Province/State: _____ Postage Code/Zip
U.S. orders payable in U.S. funds

Make cheque or money order payable to:
Doorway to Creative Cuisine Publishing
R.R. #1, Site 25
Compartment 1
Castlegar, B.C.
Canada V1N 3H7